It's a bad thing whisky,
especially
BAD WHISKY

It's a bad thing whisky,
especially

BAD WHISKY

Edward Burns

BALVAG BOOKS

First published 1995 by
BALVAG BOOKS
1/2, 7 Muirpark Street, Glasgow, G11 5NQ

© Edward Burns 1995

ISBN 0 9512020 2 2

British Library Cataloguing in Publication Data.
A catalogue record for this book is available
from the British Library.

Typeset by Newtext Composition Ltd, Glasgow
Printed in Scotland by Bell & Bain Ltd, Glasgow

Contents

Acknowledgements

I would like to thank the staff of Glasgow's Mitchell Library – and especially the Glasgow Room – for their assistance over the last few years; we got there in the end. Those employed at the following establishments have also been most helpful: Glasgow University Library; the National Library of Scotland, Edinburgh; the Ewart Library, Dumfries; Strathclyde Regional Archives; Glasgow University Archives; United Distillers Archives; the Scottish Record Office, Edinburgh; HM Customs and Excise, both in the Records Management Unit at Salford and the Personnel Directorate Division D Branch 2, London; The Scotch Whisky Association; and the Royal Pharmaceutical Society of Great Britain. In addition, my thanks go to David R. Adie of Adie Hunter, Solicitors and Notaries, 15 Newton Terrace, Glasgow.

Most of the illustrations used in this book originated in various sources within the Mitchell Library, whether from the Graham or Annan collections, or in *Trade Mark Journals* and other periodicals, and are reproduced by courtesy of the Mitchell Library. The only exceptions are the portrait of Professor Thomas Anderson (reproduced by courtesy of Glasgow University Archives), the 1870 composite photograph (reproduced by courtesy of the Royal College of Physicians and Surgeons of Glasgow), and that by the author showing 15 Newton Terrace.

Edward Burns   1995.

To the memory of
Doctor James St. Clair Gray

Introduction

VICTORIAN Glasgow, Second City of the great British Empire; an expanding Mecca of industry, with a million-and-one retailers battling to serve the needs of an ever-growing workforce. Competition was rife, and a considerable number of merchants were doing what they could to leap aboard the bandwagon of prosperity without paying their proper dues. For one group, the bubble was about to burst.

In an investigation that was to tear at the very heart of Scotland's heritage, the *North British Daily Mail* organised the sampling and analysis of whisky in public houses and illicit drinking-dens. The inquiry was conducted at a time when it was becoming increasingly difficult to purchase *any* article of food or drink which had not been subjected to some form of unacceptable alteration at the hands of unscrupulous traders. The results were astounding.

Of the thirty samples taken, only two were found to be genuine whisky. Some had nothing more harmful than water as a diluent, but others contained ingredients like turpentine, methylated spirits, sulphuric acid, and, in the worst cases, were made entirely from a thin varnish. The latter, commonly called 'finish', was legitimately used by furniture polishers and manufacturers of hats.

Such was the ensuing public outcry that the 'Mail was inundated with letters, and their pages over the following months carried either words of congratulations for the revelation or criticism of the manner in which the whole inquiry, and especially the analysis, had been conducted. This had never been heard of before! Methylated spirits couldn't possibly be added to whisky! How on earth could shellac gum be found in Scotland's national drink? ... and so it continued.

But the facts were there. Evidence from other sources eventually backed up the results. Naphtha (the source of methyl alcohol used in methylated spirits) *had* previously been detected in whisky, as had sulphuric acid, and no matter how long the arguments raged on, there was simply no doubt that some of Glasgow's whisky was grossly and intentionally contaminated, solely for profit.

Distillers were, on the whole, blameless as far as adulteration is concerned, although there are records of one in Scotland experimenting with methylic spirit in the 1850s in an attempt to add a somewhat different flavour to his product. While initially the taste was apparently passable, this little concoction (with one gallon being added to a thousand of whisky) was thankfully found to be quite unpalatable after lying for only two months, and never saw the light of day. No, it was retailers, usually of second and third-rate concerns, who were the main culprits.

In the pages that follow we will take a look at the extent of adulteration in food and drink in the mid-Victorian period, the at times astonishing disclosures providing a suitable backdrop to the mysterious goings-on in Glasgow. To facilitate a better understanding of the city's whisky problem I have also examined the general abuse of spirits, a topic that includes the sale and control of methylated spirits, the flagrant misuse of alcohol by druggists, and the dark and seedy side of the shebeen where all manner of potions were dispensed to unwary patrons.

The section dealing with druggists may at first glance seem superfluous, but they played a key role in the scenario, a lot of their spirituous business being carried out within legal guidelines that were often confusing and misunderstood, sometimes deliberately. In addition to supplying most, if not all, of the substances employed in the adulteration of food and drink, they did a roaring trade in so-called 'medicines', some of which were conspicuously sold under titles like 'Whiskee' and 'Brandee'.

This book charts the events surrounding one particular controversy connected with adulteration. It was, naturally, of great importance to the whisky industry, but when viewed in the context of the world of food and drink it was but one battle in a war that continues to this day.

1

The Beginning

Glasgow. 1872.

The air was warm, thick and acrid. August had been and gone, and summer's dying rays filtered through a heavy smog to partly illuminate the city and all her inhabitants.

Hustle and bustle.

Wooden, iron-rimmed wheels poured over wet cobbles as a thousand carts and waggons of every shape and form passed between jobs; some to the docks, some from the docks, between warehouse and factory, store and stack, a loud and veritable hive of industry. Noxious fumes emanating from works in the area of Dobbie's Loan found no escape skywards and drifted at head-height right into the centre in a sea of pollution which caused the fittest of lungs to cry out in despair.

Doctor Charles Cameron grasped his companion's arm; it was not a good day to be out and about and they were as well inside. They wove their way along Argyle Street, into the Trongate and, leaving the hazy realms of a narrow wynd behind, entered a public house.

The flickering flare of gas barely helped to lift the air of oppression as the pair felt their way to one of many wooden compartments leading off the bar and made themselves as comfortable as was possible in an atmosphere in which tobacco-smoke and smog battled for supremacy.

"Now then gents, what'll it be?"

A plump and jovial barman appeared as if by magic behind the counter, hands on hips, his face looking rosy and eager to serve, with just a hint of 'I'm a busy man, so hurry up!'

Cameron stood up, removed his hat – a rather tattered specimen which was not his own and was worn solely for effect – and wiped the beads of perspiration that made his forehead sting slightly. That's not just sweat, he thought, the Sanitary Department has got to do something about that damn chemical works; it's more than a nuisance.

"Two glasses of whisky please," he announced. "House Blend."

"Right you are gentlemen. Coming right up."

The barman made a great show of meticulously measuring a certain volume of spirit from one of a number of large wooden casks that rested at the far end of the counter, and gingerly carried the fruits of his endeavours to where the order had been placed, with so much care that each glass undoubtedly contained the meaning of life.

Money changed hands.

Cameron made a mock survey of the surrounding room. He wasn't at all interested, but was trying his best to look natural; not to appear surprised at the grime which coated every surface; nor at the drunken women who fell in through the door at regular intervals and left shortly afterwards with a well-worn vessel full of whisky. This was most certainly a new experience, and one which he was beginning to feel just a bit uncomfortable with.

Satisfied that the barman was engrossed in the serving of other customers, he turned to his companion.

"Okay. Sample Eight."

His friend produced a small glass bottle from beneath his jacket and removed the stopper. Cameron checked that the number on the paper label matched the details in his notebook and, glancing anxiously up at the counter, poured the untouched contents of his glass into the container.

The steady murmur of voices which buzzed from every angle came to a sudden lull and both men looked up, fearing they might have been rumbled, but no one stared in their direction and the background sound just as swiftly erupted once more into that expected from a raucous howff.

"Well, that's us. Let's get these to Doctor Gray."

With one full and one empty glass remaining on the table, they hurriedly left to become embroiled, unbeknown to them, in a long and bitter battle.

The Mysteries of Glasgow Whisky had just begun.

2

A Climate of Adulteration

IN August 1871 *The Food Journal* reported that the system of 'defrauding the public by the sale of spurious articles of food' was 'largely on the increase; so much so, that it is next to impossible, at least in the poorer and more densely populated districts of great cities, and in the various villages and hamlets of these islands, to obtain a pure sample of things which Nature originally made for man.'[1] In June 1872 the same journal stated that the evil was 'as rampant and even more widely spread than ever.'[2] Clearly from this, and other contemporary articles, adulteration was not a practise solely confined to a minority of unscrupulous traders, but was indeed practically ubiquitous, at least where the poorer working classes were concerned.

The sale of articles which are not quite what they appear to be was not then a new thing and stems from time immemorial when man first found himself in a position to be able to sell and barter. There was always someone who would buy that almost rotting side of beef or that barrel of beer that wasn't really beer at all but nevertheless got you good and drunk. We never learn, and it was due to a desire, if not a necessity, to protect members of the public that in 1855 the Government ordered an inquiry. The Select Committee of the House of Commons which was appointed to examine the adulteration of food, drink, and drugs stated what was already common knowledge in that 'adulteration widely prevails', and 'not only is the public health thus exposed to danger, and pecuniary fraud committed on the whole community, but the public morality is tainted, and the high commercial character of this country seriously lowered, both at home and in the eyes of foreign countries.[3] Something obviously had to be done.

While the recommendations made by this committee were a step in the right direction, and did provide much fuel upon which the 1860

Act for Preventing the Adulteration of Articles of Food or Drink was based, they fell far short of the mark required to make a serious indent on the problem and received much criticism from various quarters. *The Lancet* disagreed with the recommendation to attach punishments only to cases where the adulterants were of a toxic nature. This was, naturally, a serious area, but it meant that the greater proportion of adulteration which took place in the country would be allowed to continue unabated and would be given a 'positive legal license'. It also forced the issue of what is and what is not toxic, and would open the door to much legal wrangling over the definition. The 1860 Act itself was seriously flawed and unworkable but, again, a partial step in the right direction.

The range of adulterants varied greatly, from water and other harmless ingredients designed to expand the volume or weight of a product by the addition of a cheaper and bulkier filler, to those that were lethal. An example of the latter took place in Bradford in 1858. Joseph Neal, a lozenge manufacturer who was in the habit of adulterating his wares, sent a messenger to the nearby town of Shipley to collect an order of 'daff' from Charles Hodgson, a druggist. 'Daff' was apparently a slang term for plaster of Paris, used to conceal the real title from onlookers. In an error which was to cost the lives of at least twenty people and make some two hundred youngsters very ill, Charles Hodgson's assistant, William Goddard, supplied the messenger with twelve pounds of arsenic! Back at Bradford the poison was mixed with other ingredients to make forty pounds of lozenges, each sweet containing enough arsenic to kill two people. Thankfully, after what was a small number of deaths in comparison with what could have happened, the blunder was discovered and an even more catastrophic disaster prevented.[4]

The general situation with regard to adulteration was so bad that at times the adulterants themselves were adulterated. Cayenne pepper was commonly used to give bite to diluted gin. To prevent the pepper from becoming bleached on exposure to light, red lead could be added, as could coloured sawdust, common salt and brick-dust.[5] Lead is highly toxic and cases of lead paralysis are said to have occurred as a direct result of contaminated cayenne pepper.[6]

In an enterprising step in which it was expected to make enormous profit following the Government's 1855 inquiry and the increased media coverage of the time, the London Unadulterated Food Company sprang up. The company had the backing of a number of eminent men including directors, bankers, solicitors, general managers, and a chief analyst, and it was generally felt that adulteration would surely be near an end. The public would not risk ill health through the devious mixtures which permeated their lives – here was a source of pure, unaltered produce. The press went wild. 'A company organised,' said the *Post* , 'under the most respectable auspices for the reparation of a great social evil *must* answer well as a commercial speculation.' The *Court Circular* stated that it was a 'great comfort to feel that at last there is a fair prospect of escaping the hands of the poisoners, and of obtaining food that is neither deadly nor disgusting.'[7] Unfortunately it is not known what happened to the London Unadulterated Food Company, but it is known that their effect on the problem was practically non-existent. Adulteration was here to stay.

Dairy House of Horrors
The most common form of adulteration where liquids are concerned is, naturally, the addition of water, and in the mid-Victorian period milk suffered greatly at the hands of dealers who made profits to the detriment of their customers' health. Water in itself is not harmful, but the practice of milk dilution was so prevalent that the health of infants, the main recipient of this essential body-building fluid, was put in jeopardy. In 1877 the sanitary inspector for St. Luke's Parish in Chelsea purchased a quart of milk which was found to contain twenty-six per cent water. This amount was said to 'render it unfit for the food of children and invalids.'[8]

Where the dilution was excessive, some means had to be found to restore thickness and make the adulteration less obvious, and it was generally thought that the brains of sheep, calves, horses, and other animals were employed for this purpose. It is hard to believe that such a ghastly notion was not based on some fragment of truth, no matter how small. Nevertheless, a large number of specimens were examined in the 1850s with no brains being discovered, much to the presumed relief of the whole country.[9]

One wonders just how far milk could be diluted before it was felt that further adulteration was necessary for artificial thickness. It is reported that in 1883 the contractor who supplied milk to the 3rd Regiment of the Line, at Ship Street Barracks in Dublin, sold a mixture of one gallon of milk to nearly two-and-a-half gallons of water. Doctor

---

" THE IMPROVED "

FLUID EXTRACT OF

A N N A T T O,

For imparting a PURE *and* BEAUTIFUL
Colour to Butter and Cheese.

This " Improved " Fluid which has received the approval of the highest authorities, is *Purely vegetable,* and offers great advantages over *Annatto* in other forms.

It is perfectly soluble and mixes readily, imparting the best shade of colour with great uniformity and economy, and entire freedom from any contaminating matter.

☞ *Labels in various Languages for Export Orders.*

DIRECTIONS.

A Table-spoonful will impart a rich cowslip tint to quarter of a hundred-weight of Butter; it may be added previous to churning to as much cream as will yield that quantity. A lighter tint may be produced by lessening the quantity.

For CHEESE.—A wine-glassful will be sufficient to colour one hundred-weight. For thin Cheese use only half the quantity.

PREPARED BY

M'MASTER, HODGSON & CO.,
British Annatto Works, Dublin.

☞ OBSERVE—That the Jar should always be kept in an upright position, and shaken before used.

Although used as an accepted additive with butter and cheese, annatto probably also found its way into diluted milk where its rich hue would have disguised the bluish tinge of adulteration. (*Mitchell Library*).

Charles A. Cameron, Dublin's public analyst, carried out the analysis and found adulteration with two-hundred-and-forty-three per cent of water, for which the contractor was fined £20. 'Milk' of this nature must have been very thin indeed.[10]

In some areas the quality of water was so bad that thickening matter was already present. Well-water near a graveyard on Hampstead Hill was tested around 1856 and found to contain 'upwards of 100 grains of solid matter in the imperial gallon – due to the decomposition of animal matter in the neighbourhood of the burial place.[11]

Retailers were always quick to come up with an excuse, sometimes genuine, but more often than not fraudulent and designed to play upon the failings of statutes in existence at the time. A milk dealer in Belfast was summoned before the Police Court for selling adulterated butter-milk. A milk inspector had made the purchase and forwarded the sample to the borough analyst who certified that it contained twenty parts of water and eighty parts of milk. The milk dealer produced a witness who stated that no water had been added to the milk. However, on further examination he said it was possible that the water might have been in the cans before the milk was placed in them. A fine of 40s plus 12s costs was imposed.[12] In another instance William Mason, of Homerton, was fined £5 for selling milk diluted to the same degree. His excuse was that he added ice during hot weather so as to preserve the life of the milk.[13] Such a novel, but nevertheless rather lame, excuse obviously failed to impress the court. Perhaps we see here the embryonic stages of what we today call low-fat milk!

Milk dealers were feeling pretty aggrieved around the 1870s. Some publicans were getting off scot-free after being brought before the courts for diluting their spirits, notably gin. There was no recognised standard of alcoholic strength for gin, and the amount of water it contained varied from place to place. You might order a gin, receive one that had added water, but because it was accepted that this was the usual strength for that particular place, no adulteration had occurred. It was a very confusing area where the law was concerned. Acts were being amended and added to every few years to take account of topics overlooked in those that went before, and no sooner had a new one been passed than its wording on any number of issues was being dissected in battles across the bench. Publicans obviously wished to see some changes as far as the addition of water was concerned, but sellers of milk were far from happy at this apparent favouritism. The *Dairyman* had this to say:

> It is, however, coming it a little too strong, for these publicans, who it would seem are anxious to compel their customers to be water drinkers to a certain extent, to attempt to get the Act so altered that *they only* shall adulterate with impunity, while all other traders, forsooth, are to be subjected to the pains and penalties deservedly attaching to dishonesty of the description named. The mere fact of these gentlemen desiring to get such a clause interpolated in the Act, plainly indicates that they have a misgiving as to the legality if not morality of supplying gin and water when gin only is asked for, and it is satisfactory to know that they are still in the same uncertain frame of mind, as the Bill, in which the ill-advised amendment was embodied, has been withdrawn, and the Act of 1875 remains in status quo.[14]

Such was the hardship of life for a publican in Victorian times that they seemingly *had* to water their beer and spirits in order to make a profit and survive. Dealers in milk were probably no different.

As with gin, milk had no statutory standard of quality to guide the courts. It was early days in the analysis of food and drink and it would take much discussion before things were put in order. The system of improving the standards of food and drink is, of course, an ongoing one, and even today small steps are being made to continue the trend set at this nascent stage.

Butter was not much better. The most common form of adulteration was when grease or tallow was added, often in excess, a typical example being reported in *The Analyst* in 1879 when Elizabeth Crawford, a shopkeeper in Seaton Carew, was summoned for infringing the Food and Drugs Act. A police-officer purchased a pound of butter of which a sample was sent to the county analyst where it was discovered that no butter was contained therein. It was composed entirely of 'fats other than butter.' The offence was admitted, but because the shopkeeper had purchased it from a wholesale merchant, had no knowledge of its true composition, and had an invoice from the wholesaler to prove purchase, the case was dismissed. The grease was, of course, impounded – all thirty-six pounds of it – but the case goes a long way towards proving the ineffective nature of existing acts.[15]

In December 1870, *The Food Journal* brought to light some new forms of adulteration, namely rag pulp and horse-bone oil. The latter was said to be an ingenious adulteration used to give weight and consistency, and to retain moisture. As this fine journal stated, it was bad enough trying to envision how rags and cloth were added to butter (images of socks on toast somehow spring strangely to mind!), but no attempt had been made to discharge the dyes, and microscopic examination revealed an array of colours including magenta, blue, brown, and others.[16] It doesn't bear thinking about.

Glasgow was no angel in such matters. Mr McKinnon, a provision dealer in the city, found himself on the wrong side of the law in 1877 when he made the mistake of selling a pound of doctored butter to an assistant sanitary inspector. This was subsequently analysed by Doctor Clark, a public analyst, and found to contain 'extraneous fat to the extent of two-thirds of its weight.' Doctor Stevenson Macadam, from Edinburgh, also tested the butter, and after using two analytical methods, one the same as Clark's, came to the conclusion that it was not adulterated. Doctor Dittmar, Professor of Chemistry in the

Andersonian University, was also of the opinion that the sample was quite sound. To settle the argument a portion was sent to Somerset House where it was determined that it was almost exclusively a fat which had been mixed up with a little milk, and not butter at all. Mr McKinnon, who must have witnessed the proceedings with some interest, was fined two guineas and the cost of the Somerset House analysis.[17]

The interesting thing about the above case is its ability to demonstrate the problems faced in analysing samples and the often conflicting opinions given by analysts. Usually more than one test was available to the chemist, and while the different avenues should all have led to the same conclusion, this was not always the case. This tendency to disagree is an important factor which will feature in our whisky mystery.

Bread, Tea, and a Hair of the Dog!
In 1876, Arthur Hill Hassall's book, *Food, its Adulterations, and the Methods for Their Detection*, listed many common items of food and drink along with their adulterants. The work was similar to his *Food and its Adulterations* which provided much information for the Government's inquiry ordered in 1855. Known adulterants of bread were given as mashed potatoes, rice, beans, rye, and Indian corn. Alum was sometimes employed so as to allow the use of damaged flour, and copper sulphate could provide a bit of colour, although it is not clear what useful colour it could give to a white or brown loaf of bread. Other adulterants which were known to be used, although evidence was said to be lacking, were barley, oat, pea flour, pipe clay, plaster of Paris, bonedust, carbonates of lime, magnesia, and soda.[18]

Alum was a common adulterant of gin and other spirits and was used to restore the transparency after too much water had been added. It found its way into many Victorian recipes including one used by a chemist in Glasgow in the 1870s for treating foot-rot in sheep.[19] Proof of its use as an adulterant in bread frequently came into print, an example being found in *The Analyst* in 1877. At Wednesbury Police Court, John Harthill was summoned for selling bread adulterated with alum. The county analyst stated that the alum had been used to enable the defendant to use damaged flour and to make a presentable loaf. In addition, it prevented 'further decomposition of the gluten and other substances in the flour.' The defendant was fined £25 and costs.[20]

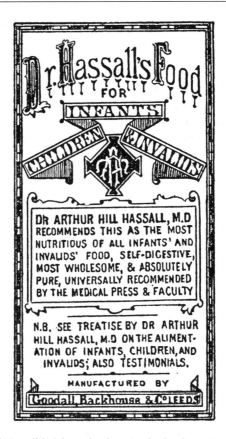

Doctor Arthur Hill Hassall led from the front in the battle against adulteration, and any product bearing his name was certainly guaranteed to be of a pure and health-giving nature. (*Mitchell Library*).

Tea found itself on both sides of the fence, often being adulterated, and occasionally playing the role of the adulterant. In 1870, a Doctor Letheby discovered what he termed 'a spurious tea' which was being shipped to this country in huge quantities – it was said that 7,000,000 pounds were due to arrive at one stage.

> This tea, which is described as 'Fine Moning Congou,' is really nothing but the re-dried leaves of the exhausted tea, the peculiar piquancy of which is increased by the fact that, in Shanghai, the pigs and dogs freely promenade amongst the rotting heaps in the streets. 'The leaves are for the most part quite rotten from the putrefactive decomposition, and do

not contain more than a trace of the active principle of tea. The odour of them is very offensive; and, when infused in boiling water, they produce a nauseous, unwholesome liquid.'[21]

I'm sure Glasgow's fine tea-rooms had none of the stuff, although a waiting market obviously existed somewhere. While worth only $1^1/2$d to $2^1/4$d per pound, the tea sold for $5^1/4$d to $7^3/4$d, its owners escaping prosecution as a result of actions taken by the Custom House authorities. In June of the same year further tea adulteration was brought to light, and samples obtained from a consignment of eighty chests revealed a variety of 'rubbish' which was being sold for $2^3/4$d per pound. Almost twenty-three per cent was made up of an array of vegetable matter of foreign origin, this concoction also containing iron filings. Yet another sample came from a green tea from India and was found to contain copper, probably derived from an attempt to give the product some colour by roasting it while in contact with copper, more than likely in copper pans. Hassall's book gives many adulterants of tea, namely exhausted tea leaves, leaves other than those of tea including sycamore, horse-chestnut and plum; lie tea, paddy husk, sand, quartz, magnetic oxide of iron, and starch. These would have been used to boost bulk and weight. For colour, the adulterator had a choice: plumbago or black lead, gum, indigo, Prussian blue, turmeric, Chinese yellow, china clay, soapstone or French chalk, mica and sulphate of lime, rose-pink, Dutch pink, vegetable red and yellow dyes, chrome yellow, Venetian red, carbonate of copper, arsenite of copper, chromate and bichromate of potash, carbonates of lime and magnesia. There must have been a veritable rainbow selection of tea available to the unwary!

On the subject of revenue, it was the responsibility of the Excise for collecting duty on tea. In the protection of the revenue it was also their responsibility to ensure that no adulterated articles on which duty was paid were allowed into public circulation. In this area they failed miserably. In the 1850s the Analytical Board of Excise had about four thousand officers scattered throughout the country, as well as sixty to seventy analytical chemists who were recruited as students educated solely for this purpose at University College. This Board was said to have failed in its principal duty. The Lancet Sanitary Commission found 'adulteration to be rife in nearly every article bearing an Excise duty, and that hundreds of adulterations were practised, and of which

The sword of purity destroys the evil serpent of adulteration in this mid-Victorian trade mark for tea. (*Mitchell Library*).

the Analytical Board of the Excise possessed no exact or scientific knowledge.[22]

By way of an interesting interjection I might say that those who cultivated tea did not have an easy life, and in times of poor harvest or adverse growing conditions it must have been very tempting to throw any old leaf into that big empty basket. On the 11th May 1855, in the vale of Kuttyoor, surrounded by lofty and frosty mountains, where the Assam shrub grew and villagers delicately picked leaves for tea drinkers worldwide, a passing storm threw down hailstones of twelve inches in circumference![23]

Green tea was an occasional adulterant of whisky. Freshly distilled whisky was very rough to the palate, and even slightly toxic, and was said to drive men wild, or fighting drunk. Because new spirit was cheaper than the old it was often used by publicans who had no scruples or fears of the effect on their customers, and sundry articles were added to disguise the flavour and make the drink more palatable. These included sherry wine, tartaric and acetic acids, sugar, pineapple and other fruit essences, tincture of prunes, acetic ether, oil of wine, spirit of nitrous ether, glycerine, and, of course, green tea, as well as other things. Another way of avoiding the effect of young or bad whisky was to drink 'Robur', a new tea-spirit which appeared in the 1870s. This was free of fusel oil, a substance which was present in young whisky and which contributed greatly to its harsh taste, and contained the 'well-known refreshing properties of tea, which is a nervine tonic, and, with the alcohol, forms a tonic stimulant, which it stands to reason must be wholesome.' It was thought that this tea-spirit might be used to wean drinkers off whisky and point them upon a path of teetotalism, and a suggestion was made to the effect that experiments could be carried out on dipsomaniacs in hospitals to test the effect of 'Robur' on their systems. It is not clear what the temperance movement thought of it all; 'Robur' *did* contain alcohol and as such there could have been little beneficial effect.[24]

The Victorian grocer's shelves were filled with countless items tainted by illicit interference. Plaster of Paris was a common adulterant of many, its weight and ease of access making it a popular additive to goods like sauces, sugar, flour, anchovies, mustard, and no doubt many others. The accumulative effect of adulterants being adulterated must have made a trip to the shops a real life-in-one's-hands expedition. The rich could pick and choose and afford to avoid goods obviously debased, while the poor did not have that choice and were subjected to the most horrific malpractices imaginable. The ever-spiraling circle of abuse sent many to an early grave. Coffee was commonly adulterated with chicory. Chicory was adulterated with sawdust, burnt blood and baked horses' liver. Spices could be expanded by adding flour. Flour was often adulterated with chalk, powdered flints, plaster of Paris, alum, and other things. Ginger could be adulterated with cayenne pepper, the latter containing, as has already been stated, red lead, a highly toxic substance which was used to provide colour to a number of articles including curry powder, cocoa and chocolate, sauces, and confectionery. The public at large were being slowly poisoned.

Sweet Marbles and Rifle Shots

If there was such a thing as a Top Ten for the most toxic adulterated food in Victorian Britain, then confectionery would be up among the top three. The disturbing aspect of this form of adulteration is that the recipients were mainly children, and no sooner had they left the cradle than they were being subjected to all manner of potentially fatal compounds. As every mother knew, although she didn't know why, a big bag of sweets often signalled a morning-after-the-night-before sort of feeling that forced the use of 'powders' or castor oil in order to put the youngster back on his or her feet. It wasn't an overdose of sugar that made the child feel unwell, but the fact that deleterious ingredients were poisoning their system.

As *The Food Journal* stated in July 1870, 'there is no more unblushing and licensed poisoner in the world, than the unscrupulous manufacturer of cheap confectionery.' As a demonstration of the extent of the problem, the journal purchased and examined various sweets in the London area. Of the one-hundred-and-five samples, thirty were red, twenty-three yellow, twelve blue, twelve brown, five green and twenty-three white, the proportions of the different colours being indicative of the popularity of each. The results were frightening. Red sweets weren't too bad; only one was coloured with red lead, and three with vermilion (mercuric sulphide), the rest were quite safe. Yellow sweets were mostly toxic. The colour should have been provided by turmeric or some other vegetable colouring, instead thirteen contained chrome-yellow (a pigment of lead chromate). Contaminated samples included names like 'Hundreds of Thousands', 'Rifle Shots', 'Sweet Marbles', 'Motto Lozenges', 'Fishes', and many others. Anyone taking a great quantity of lead-impregnated lozenges could find themselves in trouble. An instance is recorded in which someone partook of a large amount of coloured ginger lozenges to allay flatulance. Symptoms following such deadly overindulgence commence with sudden attacks of excruciating pain in the bowels, sometimes referred to as 'painters' colic'. The patient becomes worn and thin, the hands tremble, and pain is felt in the legs and feet. A paralysis then sets in, characterised by what is called 'wrist-drop', and death may follow shortly thereafter. This might seem a bit morbid, but it is a fact that children were being exposed to these horrors, their suffering cries often appeased momentarily by the very thing that was causing their ill.

Half of the blue sweets were adulterated with either copper, cobalt or ultramarine, the only pigment which should have been permissible being indigo. Iron was detected in seven of the brown sweets, and although not actively poisonous, was not recommended. The small number of green sweets echoed the public's fears as a result of previous warnings. As *The Food Journal* stated, 'nearly all the mineral greens contain copper, while the brightest one (Scheele's green) superadds the charms of arsenic to those of the former sufficiently dangerous metallic poison.'[25] Other toxic greens commonly used in confectionery were verdigris (copper acetate), copper arsenite (Scheele's green), Brunswick Green, and Zinc Green (zinc and cobalt). All the samples were adulterated and the journal instructed its readers to *never*, under any circumstances, allow such comfits to be used in their families. Nothing poisonous was detected in any of the clear or white sweets, although adulteration certainly took place, sometimes with plaster of Paris.

The use of artificial essences was also examined, the details coming from evidence brought before the Parliamentary committee subsequent to 1855. Some sweets flavoured with such essences were capable of inducing drowsiness or stupor in the eater and much of this was thought to be due to careless manufacturing practises. Although toxic in high doses, the risk was lessened considerably when the essence was properly mixed and distributed throughout the batch of sweets under production. Incorrect mixing could result in some sweets having little flavour and others carrying dangerously high levels. The essence of bitter almonds is a prime example. It usually contained a large quantity of the deadly poison prussic acid, and persons wishing to commit suicide or murder have been known to use the essence when unable to procure the pure acid. Eating too many almond-flavoured sweets would probably not cause death, but the example demonstrates the potential risk faced by countless children and the unacceptable reliance placed upon manufacturers' good working practices. One sugared almond sample was found to lack an almond (the least of its worries), was made from a mass of sugar and sulphate of lime 'slightly tinged on the surface with chrome yellow and red lead,' and contained a lot of prussic acid. This was no sweet, it was a time-bomb!

The final word on confectionery rests with *The Food Journal*:

> It may be argued that the minute quantity employed renders the poisons completely harmless; but let us remember the small and delicate little organisms into which the bulk of the sweetstuff in England is intended to pass, as well as the fact that lead arsenic and most of the pigments used are cumulative poisons, which do not leave the system, but go on collecting force, as it were, for their fatal work from each replenishment.[26]

Meat not so Sweet

From the subject of sweetmeat we now move to look very briefly at meat. There was very rarely any adulteration and it only became a problem when sold in an unwholesome or rotting condition. Inspectors of Unwholesome Meat, attached to the Sanitary Department, could enter premises to examine any 'carcass, meat, poultry, game, flesh, fish, fruit, or vegetable exposed for sale' and seize any found to be unfit for use as human food. Seizures were common, but the use of inspectors kept the offence more or less in check. Fish could be destroyed, and putrid meat might be removed from the premises and buried, at times with the owner's consent, with no prosecution. In 1871 in Glasgow the title was changed, presumably to accommodate the ever-growing concern, to Inspector of Unwholesome and Adulterated Food. The city was no different from any other in having only one man at this post, besides, there were other more pressing areas for inspectors to attend to, like belching factory chimney-fumes and other nuisances, overcrowded and unsafe lodging-houses, epidemics that were sweeping through the dense population like wildfire, unsafe workshops, unclean bakehouses, and so on. Adulterated food was a problem, but it wasn't the only one.

A rather peculiar form of adulteration reared its head in Paris in 1872. A house in the Levallois-Perret area was once home to a butcher who was executed for selling flesh from persons he had murdered for human food. Local inhabitants became rightly concerned when, once again, a disgusting and familiar smell emanated from the forbidding premises. Tongues started to wag and rumour had it that the house owner was using the discovered remains of buried communists in sausages he was preparing. A sample purchase was made and the sausage meat was found to be in 'a horrible state of decomposition.' The manufacturer, his sausages and meat, were immediately seized and such was the condition of his wares that persons carrying out the inspection were 'seized with serious vomitings'. It emerged that the meat was in fact from cats and dogs and other animals collected from the streets of Paris.[27] *The Food Journal* in June 1873 also reported an incident during some Parisian conflict in which a 'wretch' of a citizen was found selling pies made of human flesh, although thankfully this form of adulteration was not too common.

Tobacco and the Life-Saving Puff
In 1603 King James I said of the smoking of tobacco – 'A custom disgusting to the eye, hurtful to the brain, dangerous to the lungs, and, with its black stinking smoke, as like as possible to the horrible Stygian vapour of the bottomless abyss.' Many were opposed to his views and the custom grew in popularity despite his harsh criticism. In the nineteenth century the satirical writer and humorist Thomas Chandler Haliburton, while under his literary disguise of Sam Slick the Clockmaker, wrote – 'The fact is, squire, the moment a man takes to a

pipe he becomes a philosopher. It's the poor man's friend; it calms the mind, soothes the temper, and makes a man patient under difficulties. It has made more good men, good husbands, kind masters, indulgent fathers, than any other blessed thing on this universal earth.'[28]

However, it wasn't only food and drink that was adulterated, and tobacco, along with practically every saleable commodity that existed in the mid-nineteenth century, was also subjected to sundry nefarious malpractises. Substances added to increase bulk and weight include water, sugar, treacle, salts, oil, plant leaves (rhubarb, potato, coltsfoot, dock, and others), malt comings, earthy matter, sand, and no doubt many others. Also thought to have been used were the leaves of cabbage, seaweed, roasted chicory-root, bran, and oakum.[29] In 1865 the United Kingdom received 66,000,000 lbs of imported tobacco, the Great Plant now known as a prime staple of ordinary life, and it is not difficult to see that even if a relatively minor percentage of this figure was adulterated once in this country, the potential loss to the Inland Revenue was very great indeed; one barrel of tobacco made up to two with various British plant leaves meant a loss to the Government of the duty normally paid on that extra barrel, had it been imported.

Tobacco offered much more to the Victorians than just a good smoke. It was said to be a valued antiseptic. An infusion of a 'halfpenny twist of tobacco in a bottle of beer' alleviated asthmatic conditions; the same infusion was found to be a valuable remedy in the treatment of dysentry. Large dried leaves could be scented by leaving in close proximity to a mixture of musk and powdered tonka-beans for about ten days, when they could then be used to give a refreshing odour to rooms. The *British Pharmacopoeia* of 1864 has a recipe for 'Enema Tabaci', or 'Enema of Tobacco', in which twenty grains of tobacco-leaf are infused with eight fluid ounces of boiling water. A Glasgow chemist's 'Cure for Mosquitoes,' dating to the 1870s, was made from pine or juniper sawings, powdered leaves of unidentifiable origin, tobacco, and a small quantity of arsenic. While on this deadly topic, it was once thought that the Chinese used arsenic in manufacturing mosquito tobacco; either way, it seems that mosquitoes had a pretty hard time of it in those days!

Had you been a smoker in the army and wished to mask those unflattering odours of tobacco and gunpowder smoke which, while killing off hoards of fleas, made you unattractive to ladies in your company, you could avail yourself of 'Le Bombardier' – a nifty little perfume produced by a druggist in Sheffield in the 1860s. It disguised the 'odour of stale tobacco, of which the uniforms of our gallant volunteers are apt to become so redolent, making them at once presentable in the ball-room straight from the battle-field.[30] While on the subject of tobacco and its tendency to permeate clothes and the human body itself, an amusing anecdote was presented in *The Food Journal* in May 1871, in which a Captain Wilkes, during an expedition to foreign lands, interrogated a native of the Fiji Islands as to the fate of the crew of a vessel whose shattered hull still lay upon the beach... "'All kill," replied the savage. "What did you do with them?" asked Captain Wilkes. "Eat 'em. Good," returned the cannibal. "Did you eat them all?" inquired the half-sick captain. "All but one," holding up a finger. "And why did you spare one?" "Cause him taste *too like tobacco*; couldn't eat him no how."'

Tobacco and beer have always been linked, the thought of their harmonious alliance evoking images of pewter mutchkins of ale combined with long-stemmed pipes in the peaceful atmosphere of an old public house. At one time tobacco was one of many adulterants of beer, reputedly used for its narcotic or soporific effect in place of hops. The clay tobacco pipe was also a useful tool in determining if your beer was pure or grossly contaminated. The end would be heated to red hot in an open fire and then plunged into the suspect liquid until cool. If, on removal, the clay was still white, then it was safe to finish your beer. If, on the other hand, it emerged black or cloudy and obviously coated with some peculiar matter, your beer had been adulterated and you were advised never to return to that same howff.

Beer and the Doctor

Before hops were used to provide taste, aroma, and keeping quality to beer, broom-tops, wormwood, and other bitter plants were employed. Each struggled for survival for several hundred years until around 1700 when the hop became the predominant bitter ingredient. In the early eighteenth century brewers were forbidden to mix 'sugar, honey, Guinea-pepper, essentia bina, cocculus indicus, or any other unwholesome ingredients' in beer, and it may be assumed from this that there were some who were apt to do so.[31] In 1802 an act was passed which disallowed the use of any substance in brewing other than malt, hops and water; later legislation then permitted the use of sugar, first in a burnt form for colouring porter, and then for the brewing of beer. Scant regard was paid to the 1802 Act and most beers at that time were, according to one contemporary writer, 'only a composition of drugs' and other poisonous constituents like 'Grains of Paradise', quassia, tobacco, lime, and countless others. The coriander seed was also used and mentioned in A *Practical Treatise* on *Brewing*, dating to 1806 – 'For in most brewers' ales, etc., they put in the coriander seed, and though a tasteless berry, yet nothing is so poisonous and stupifying a quality; and one pound of this seed, will be equal in strength, to a bushel or two of malt, guinea pepper, opium, etc.'[32]

Cocculus indicus was illegally used as a substitute for malt and hops and is the fruit or berry of the *Anamirta paniculata*, a large tree native to the coast in the areas of Malabar and Ceylon. The pea-sized fruit contains between one and two per cent of the poisonous alkaloid picrotoxin to which it owes its narcotic properties. In increasing the inebriating qualities of beer, it also exposed the drinker to bouts of nausea, vomiting, 'and griping pains, followed by stupor and intoxication.'[33] The following recipe for porter dates to around the beginning of the nineteenth century.[34]

> 1 quarter of malt. 8lbs of hops. 9lbs of treacle. 8lbs of liquorice root. 8lbs of essentia bina. 8lbs of colour. Capsicum, half an ounce. Spanish liquorice, two ounces. Cocculus indicus, a quarter of an ounce. Salt of tartar, two drachms. Heading. Ginger, three ounces. Lime, four ounces. Linseed, one ounce. Cinnamon, two drachms.

In 1816 an act was passed which said that no brewer was allowed to mix, add, or have in his possession, any 'Molasses, Honey, Liquorice, Vitriol, Quassia, Coculus Indiae, Grains of Paradise, Guinea Pepper, or Opium,'[35] the actual statute being very long-winded and designed to ensure that all potential loopholes were covered. They were, but it didn't stop adulteration. Minutes of the Committee of the House of Commons around this period contain lists of publicans prosecuted and convicted for receiving and using illegal ingredients in their brewing. The following was seized from a Mr Nibbs on July 12th 1817.[36]

Multum	– 84lbs
Cocculus Indicus	– 12lbs
Colouring	– 4 gallons

Honey	– 180 lbs
Hartshorn shavings	– 14lbs
Spanish Juice, Orange Powder, Ginger.	

In 1834 a druggist's book revealed dealings in over 2,500 bags of *Cocculus indicus*, most of which would have gone to brewers.[37] The 1855 Parliamentary inquiry into adulteration also looked at beer, and the evidence provided by Mr P. L. Simmonds was that at least 250 tons of the drug was imported each year, chiefly for the use of brewers.[38]

There were many adulterants of beer. The above-mentioned inquiry put the following question to a Mr Edwin Wickham: 'Do you believe that the adulteration of beer is a common thing?', to which he replied, 'Very common, so much so that the exception is not to adulterate; and I believe those exceptions are very few.' He went on to say, 'From my experience in brewing I believe that the great adulteration of beer takes place in the cellars of the publicans and not in the breweries, although I know it is done by some brewers.' Mr Wickham then gave the following recipe for the adulteration of porter, as used by many publicans:

> To one barrel of porter eight gallons of water, six pounds of sugar, one pound of gelatin (or patent size will do), a handful of common salt, extract of *gentian* or *quassia* to restore to it the original bitter flavour, *sulphate of ammonia* to bring it back to its colour, half an ounce of *sulphate of iron*, and if required to taste oldish, an ounce of *roche alum*.'[39]

The bulk of beer adulteration was carried out to give colour, taste, and bite to liquor greatly diluted with water. Publicans seemingly had no choice but to water their wares, such was the retail price compared with that charged by the brewers.[40] No profit meant no business. With a bit of trickery in the privacy of a cool cellar, the publican could magically transform two barrels into three, the unfortunate effect being that the beer now looked and tasted watered-down. Things were added to make this less obvious.

On the harmless side, burnt sugar was used to restore colour, while the addition of salt increased the pungency and flavour, not to mention the obvious beneficial spin-off of giving the drinker a thirst for more. A mixture of brown sugar and treacle – called 'Foots' – was often added to restore colour and sweetness, as was, in the case of porter, Spanish

This 1877 trade mark promotes tea as a safe alternative to the destructive powers of alcohol. (*Mitchell Library*).

juice or liquorice. The previously-mentioned 'essentia bina' was sugar boiled down to a dark colour and rich, burnt flavour, and this imparted a perfect mask to the reality behind the glass.

A variety of vegetable bitters was used to restore taste, including chiretta, wormwood, orange-peel, orange-powder, camomile, and, as has already been mentioned, quassia and gentian, the chief sale of the latter in this country being in fact to publicans.[41] Some of these also had a slight narcotic effect which allowed the villainous publican to cover his tracks in two areas – taste and strength.

Around 1850 a number of English newspapers carried reports that strychnine was used extensively in the brewing industry. The story originated in Paris where it was said that large quantities of the poison

31

were manufactured and exported to England for use in the brewing of bitter beers and pale ales. Although giving a bitter taste to the beer in very small amounts, the poison is cumulative and continued small doses could build up in the body with serious consequences. The brewers were furious. While strychnine may have been used by a tiny number of devious persons, it was *all* brewers of bitter beer who were tainted by the story, and so two major firms, Messrs Allsopp & Sons and Messrs Bass & Co, offered their wares for analysis. The results revealed nothing more in the beer than malt, hops, and 'pure spring water', and one has to wonder whether the spreading of this malicious rumour wasn't perhaps a ploy to increase sales of French wines. Incidentally, in 1857 the *Lebanon Star* reported the deaths of four men from drinking whisky which contained strychnine. This was presumably some sort of horrendous mistake – quite unimaginable – that also caused the demise of tens of thousands of fish in the stream below the distillery.[42]

'Grains of Paradise' were used extensively to give diluted beer an artificial strength. These hot, pungent, cardamom-like seeds were imported in vast quantities and used entirely in the adulteration of beer and spirits. The addition of iron sulphate gave the beer froth and a head, and imparted a metallic smartness. In 1817 310lbs of this chemical were seized from a druggist who supplied brewers and public houses. Sulphuric acid was frequently added to 'bring beer forward' and to make a new brew taste like an eighteen month-old veteran. The 'heading' alluded to in the previous recipe for porter was a mixture of 'half alum and half copperas, ground to a fine powder; and is so called from giving to porter the beautiful head of froth which constitutes one of its peculiar properties, and which landlords are so anxious to raise to gratify their customers.'[43] Other peculiar substances that found their way into beer were beans, 'multum' (another name for *Cocculus indicus*), ginger, and oyster shells, the latter used to recover sour beer.

Such was the extensive range of illicit additives available to the Victorian publican that it must have been quite a confusing affair trying to decide which to use when and with what beer. To the uninitiated the whole process must have looked like mystical hocus-pocus reminiscent of the age of alchemists and the like, and for some the only cure for 'sick' beer was to call in 'The Doctor'. The 'Beer-Doctor', as he came to be known, was a well-known character whose services included the visiting of hostelries to administer remedies to

The sour or acidic taste of stale beer could be counteracted by 'Sleight's Publicans' Friend', one of many substances available to the licensing trade from chemists and druggists. (*Mitchell Library*).

'sick' beer.[44] Chances are he was probably a travelling brewers' druggist taking orders and offering advice to bemused publicans who were desirous of an instant solution to the bad or over-diluted beer which they hoped to sell the following day. The practised hands would introduce some of this and some of that, and before you could say 'mutchkin of mild' men were quaffing it like there was no tomorrow, calling it a great brew, and getting very very drunk. To the working man, who lived in dank, dreary housing, the public house was his palace, and on a Friday night he didn't really care what was in his glass, as long as it tasted reasonably like beer and made him intoxicated.

At times the brewers' druggist made no attempt to conceal his identity and the obvious nefarious practises he carried out, and practically cocked a snoot at the law by leaving his cart, complete with his name and designation, standing in front of a public house in broad daylight. Evidence heard during the 1855 Inquiry revealed that two of the largest druggists in London constantly sold *Cocculus indicus*, 'Foots' sugar, liquor ammoniae, and extract of gentian to publicans.

The 1872 Act for Regulating the Sale of Intoxicating Liquors (The Licensing Act, for short) made a further attempt to stem the tide of

33

liquor abuse (although it was not extended to Scotland) and was passed at the same time – 10th August 1872 – as the Act to Amend the Law for the Prevention of Adulteration of Food and Drink and Drugs. Clearly moves were being made to tackle the problem from all angles. The Licensing Act made it an offence for any person to make or keep adulterated liquor, and anyone found guilty was liable to a maximum fine of £20 or one month in prison, with or without hard labour. Should a second offence be committed, the fine was raised to £100 maximum or three months imprisonment, and the unfortunate malefactor was declared to be 'a disqualified person for a period of not less than two years nor exceeding ten years.' In the case of publicans, this meant losing their licence. No deleterious ingredients were allowed to be kept on the premises, and these were listed as 'Cocculus indicus, chloride of sodium otherwise common salt, copperas, opium, Indian hemp, strychnine, tobacco, darnel seed, extract of logwood, salts of zinc or lead, alum, and any extract or compound of any of the above ingredients.' The adulteration amendment Act tackled the overall problem, including beer, and any person who wilfully mixed any injurious or poisonous ingredient, or any material, with articles of food, drink, or drugs, for the purposes of adulteration, was liable to a £50 fine or, on the second offence, six months hard labour. Woe betide anyone who broke the law, but, of course, the difficulty was in detection and conviction, and it would be quite some time before any real roads were driven through this legal mine-field.

Getting into the Spirit of Things
Gin, or geneva (to give it its full and seldom-used title), is a spirit distilled from grain, which is rectified and then flavoured with juniper berries or other aromatic substances. It was also called Hollands at one time after its place of origination in the distilleries of Schiedam.

Incorrect rectification could give an impure spirit containing fusel-oil, a substance of heterogeneous character whose undesirable qualities made the spirit nauseous and the drinker fighting drunk. In the 1850s much of the gin sold in London was of this ilk, and was said to arise through the use of 'the damaged grain which abounds after a moist autumn;' – 'Such spirits intoxicate more strongly than pure spirits of the same strength, and excite in many persons even temporary frenzy.'[45] This was not true adulteration, the chemistry and effects of fusel-oil were little understood and in an early stage of discovery, but nevertheless, incomplete rectification or the deliberate use of damaged grain was certainly not good practise.

As well as juniper berries, a number of things could be added, depending on the required final taste, and these included coriander, cardamom, caraway seeds, 'Grains of Paradise', angelica root, calamus root, crushed almond cake, liquorice powder, and orange peel. Combinations of some of these can be seen in the following recipes.[46]

Plain, or London Gin:

> 700 gallons of the second rectification
> 70 lbs juniper-berries
> 70 lbs coriander-seeds
> $3^1/2$lbs almond-cake
> $1^1/2$lb angelica-root
> 6 lbs liquorice powder.

Geneva – The charge of still being 950 gallons of the second rectification, the proportions are:

> 84 lbs juniper-berries
> 112lbs coriander-seeds
> 6 lb cassia-buds
> 4 lbs angelica-root
> 6 lbs calamus-root
> 6 lbs almond-cake
> $1/2$ lb cardamum

When not tampering with barrels of beer, the Victorian publican was tinkering with his gin, and even if it arrived at his premises in pretty good condition you can be sure that by the time it reached the mouths of his customers it contained all manner of peculiar ingredients. Water was, once again, the main adulterant and acted like a primer by demanding the addition of further adulterants to disguise its presence. Subsequent additions caused problems of their own, the only remedy being to introduce even more foreign substances, and before long what started out as an alcoholic drink had become a measure of poison.

There was much debate about the strength of gin and the amount of water it could contain before it was said to be adulterated. The strength varied from place to place, and some people were being fined for adding water while others were brought before the courts for the same offence and dismissed with no charge. Two cases in 1878 demonstrate the ambiguous nature of judges in different parts of the country. At Stockton, five innkeepers were charged with selling adulterated gin. A pint of gin, purchased by an inspector from Joseph Tynan, was analysed and found to be 43 under proof. The solicitor for the defence submitted that no conviction should follow if it could be proved that the gin in question was of the strength usually sold in the district. A witness was then called to prove that the gin was bought at 22 under proof, and that 20 per cent of water was customarily added, this being the innkeepers' only way of making a profit. The case, along with the remaining four, was dismissed. However, at Bishop Auckland, Hugh Stoker was charged with selling gin at 49 under proof. With the aim of obtaining a conviction, Superintendent Henderson had entered the inn and asked for a pint of gin. Sensing trouble, Mr Stoker drew some from a cask that had just come in and which he had presumably not got around to diluting. The superintendent refused this and asked for a pint from another cask, to which he pointed. 'This,' said Mr Stoker, 'is gin and water'. His admission, which was intended to reveal the true nature of the cask's contents (it was not an offence to sell gin and water, just as long as it was called, and labelled, 'gin and water', and not solely 'gin'), was not enough. He was fined £5 and had his licence endorsed. These two cases opened the door to a great deal of discussion on the subject.[47]

Over-diluted gin tended to go turbid due to precipitation of the oily and resinous material of the juniper berry and other flavouring substances, and steps had to be taken to put this right. Alum, carbonate of potash, and acetate of lead were used for clarification, the latter partly remaining in the spirit thus rendering it poisonous. Sulphuric acid might also be added as part of a mixture containing the above-mentioned alum and carbonate of potash, along with almond-oil and spirits of wine, and this not only fined the gin but communicated to it 'the property of 'beading', or hanging in pearly drops or beads on the sides of the glass containing it. When gin does this, it is generally supposed to be strong in proportion as it beads, and the above mixture communicates to weak gin that property, so that it will be evident gin can be considerably diluted with water, and yet, by the addition of the above, appear of its proper strength.'[48]

The gin might now look good, but in the department of taste it failed miserably. To remedy this, sugar, cayenne pepper, or 'Grains of Paradise' were added. Of thirty-eight samples of gin analysed in the 1870s, seven were found to contain very large quantities of cayenne pepper, so much so that on evaporation the syrupy extract that remained 'possessed a burning and fiery taste.' As Hassall stated in his 1876 book – 'The introduction into the stomach of raw spirits is sufficiently destructive to health of itself, but the addition to the spirit of such powerful and acrid substances as Cayenne and grains of paradise forms a compound which no human stomach or system, however strong, can long withstand.'[49]

Of course this fiery pepper not only irritated the stomach but contained hidden, intrusive toxins like red lead. Adulteration was a vicious wheel which gathered momentum with every illicit addition and threatened the lives of the lower classes. A reasonably well-dressed gent could command the respect of a publican, probably for no other reason than the notion that he might be an official, and would be served the 'good' gin, not the hotchpotch dished up to the masses. And the strange thing about it all was the apparent total ignorance of the problem by the Excise. Evidence given before the Parliamentary inquiry set up in 1855 heard a Mr George Phillips respond to the query of what the Excise was doing to tackle the issue of adulteration in public houses, with the following reply: 'The fact is, we have abandoned what is termed stock-taking of the retailers. The trade is thrown open, and they are left to do pretty much as they like.' He was then asked if he had ever heard of cayenne pepper being mixed with gin, to which he replied, 'I have *heard* so; it could be detected, of course;' and to the question, 'Have you never had any experience of the adulteration of spirits during the twelve years you have spoken of?' – 'I do not recollect a case.'[50] As Hassall said, 'These replies certainly evince an amount of ignorance of the adulteration occurring in the articles enumerated, which, considering the position and duties of the Excise, is really astounding.'

Other spirits were subjected to similiar practises. Brandy is a spirit distilled from wine, generally from refuse wines or the murk left in the wine-press, or, in the case of Cognac, from those of a superior quality. It could be fraudulently made with spirits obtained from potatoes, the problem here being the presence of fusel-oil if the spirit had received poor rectification. A lot of the French brandy imported into this country was made partly, if not wholly, from beetroot spirit, and it may have been this which inspired the Excise to carry out experiments in 1871/72 to determine the viability of obtaining spirits from this plant.

Spurious French brandy might be obtained from corn spirit, diluted to proof strength, and treated in the following way: 'to every hundredweight of the spirit, half a pound of *argol, wine-stone, or cream of tartar* previously dissolved in water, is added, as well as a little *acetic ether*, some French *wine vinegar*, bruised *French plums*, and *flower stuff* from Cognac (murk). The spirit is then to be distilled off, with a gentle fire, in an alembic furnished with an agitator. The spirit which comes over is coloured with burnt sugar to the tint required, and roughened to the taste with a few drops of the tincture of *catechu* or *kino*.'[51]

Catechu is a dark extract from various Indian plants which is rich in tannin. In *Chemical Testing of Wines and Spirits*, by Griffin, a sample of public house brandy was analysed and found to contain 'a quantity of *tannin* so large as to become almost like ink when mixed with a salt of iron.' This was not a distilled spirit, according to Griffin, and was a bit of a puzzle until he read in a German book the following instructions for manufacturing Cognac: 'Take of acetic ether ³/4lb., spirit of nitric ether ¹/2lb., French wine 8 quarts, oak-bark tincture (made with ¹/4lb. of oak bark and ¹/2 quart of spirit) ¹/2 quart, purified spirit so much as to bring the whole to 150 quarts of 54 per cent. Tralles.'[52] After a lengthy period of storage, this amalgam was seemingly very similar to real Cognac in taste and odour. Other illicit ingredients were oak sawdust, tincture of grape stones, cherry laurel water, spirit of almond cake, the now familiar 'Grains of Paradise' and, to a much lesser extent, cayenne pepper.

Rum was no different. At its best it should have been a spirit obtained from the fermented skimmings of the juice of the sugar-cane mixed with molasses, at worst it was the usual diluted nightmare containing cayenne pepper, *Cocculus indicus* and, in some cases, lead, although the latter was thought to be accidental contamination derived from part of the distillation process. In 1829 several sailors became very ill after drinking one glass of rum heavily impregnated with *Cocculus indicus*. One subsequently died that evening.

A Wee Dram

When one considers the extent of the adulteration problem and the examples previously listed in this chapter, it would clearly be very surprising if whisky was not subjected to similar malpractises. Of course it has often been said that the spirit has marvellous medicinal properties, and before delving back into the deeds of despair it may be of some interest and amusement to take a look at great words of wisdom from Hollinshed's *Chronicles* of 1577 …

> Beying moderately taken, sayeth he, it sloweth age; it strengtheneth youthe; it helpeth digestion; it cutteth fleume; it abandoneth melancholie; it relisheth the harte; it lighteneth the mynd; it quickneth the spirites; it cureth the hydropsie; it healeth the strangury; it pounceth the stone; it repelleth grauel; it puffeth awaie ventositie; it kypeth and preserveth the hed from whyrlyng – the eyes from dazelyng; the tongue from lispyng; the mouthe from snafflyng; the teethe from chatteryng – the throte from ratlyng; the weasan from stieflyng; the stomache from wamblyng; the harte from swellyng – the bellie from wirtchyng; – the guts from rumblyng; the hands from shiueryng; the sinowes from shrinkyng; the veynes from crumplyng; the bones from akyng; the marrow from soakyng… And trulie it is a soueraigne liquor, if it be orderlie taken.[53]

Whisky was not known as *aquavitae* (the water of life) for nothing! Records mention it in Scotland as far back as the late fifteenth century, and it wasn't until just after the time of Bonnie Prince Charlie and the 1745 Rebellion that it crept down from its Highland home to titillate the palates of those in the Lowlands.

There are two basic types of whisky. The first is the more traditional malt whisky distilled from malted barley in a pot-still. The second is grain whisky distilled from maize, rye, buckwheat, oats, and other raw grains mixed with about one-tenth its weight of malted barley. Since the invention of Aeneas Coffey's patent-still in the 1830s, most grain whisky has been produced using this quicker and cheaper method, the only drawbacks being that the spirit, although purer and of higher strength, lacks the oils and aromatic substances that gives whisky (and especially malt) its body and flavour. Grain whisky *has* been made using the pot-still, but the practise died out around the First World War. Patent-still whisky is mainly used in blends and acts as a diluent of the more powerful properties of malt whisky.

From the mid-nineteenth right up to the twentieth century there was much talk about whether this product of the patent-still could rightly be called whisky as it had none of the usual characteristics of malt whisky, and was termed a silent spirit. Pot-still whisky was not without its problems either. Its very essence was the taste and aroma redolent of peat and all the good things that made Scotland Scottish, not to mention the essential compounds, most present in minute traces, which combined to give the whisky of each and every still its unique identity. Fusel-oil was the problem. The whisky is distilled twice, first in a wash-still to produce 'low wines', and then in a spirit-still. During this latter distillation, only the middle portion of the distillate is retained as whisky, the first bit (foreshot) and the last (feints) are returned to go through the whole process again with another batch. This final portion, or feints, contains fusel-oil, which is, without getting too technical, a generic term which covers for a whole host of constituents including amyl alcohol and other oily compounds. Although most of the fusel-oil in the feints is not included in the final whisky, some does get through, and without it whisky would almost certainly not be whisky at all. It is initially noxious and completely ruins the taste of the spirit, but after a period of storage in wooden casks it gradually changes into harmless chemicals that add considerably to the nose.

Come, a' ye torn-doon, ragged crew,
Wi' shaky limbs an' runckl'd broo,
Wi' stomach riddled wi' the dew,
    Sing praise o' Foosel Oil, O!

Come ye wha are your country's scorn,
Wha cause baith wife and bairns to mourn;
Nae mair ye'll taste John Barleycorn, –
    He's droon'd in Foosel Oil, O!

Wi' blue-anes through your brains sae rife,
Ye draw upon your frien' a knife,
An' ye wha thump your starvin' wife,
    Sing praise o' Foosel Oil, O!

The debate about patent-still grain whisky, fusel-oil and its toxicity, and the length of time which whisky should be stored and matured, culminated in an inquiry by a Select Committee of the House of Commons in 1890, and this in turn led to a Royal Commission in 1908/09, but it wasn't until the First World War that legislation was

X RAYS
Chaste Old
MEDICINAL WHISKY

This Whisky is an old production - in unison with the latest scientific discoveries – embodying unusual Natural Medicinal Properties, affecting beneficially the Spleen, Liver, and Kidneys, for relieving Gout, Rheumatism &c. it has special claims on Consumers, besides being a most wholesome & reliable stimulant for general use.

NOTE – To ensure economical distribution consumers are respectfully requested to name this Whisky to friends.

Under very close scrutiny, this whisky had nothing to hide, its medicinal properties being pushed by reference to numerous ailments said to benefit from its consumption. (*Mitchell Library*).

41

passed prohibiting the sale of whisky that had been matured for less than three years. Incidentally, as part of the above inquiry, experiments were carried out on monkeys. Two were used. The first was made drunk with new whisky and was seen to become quarrelsome, no doubt due to the fusel-oil (which was well-known for making men fighting-drunk), and the second was intoxicated with 'fine old whisky' with the result that it became 'markedly hilarious', the maturity and lack of toxic ingredients obviously agreeing with the chimp. Once sobered-up, the experiment was reversed causing the quarrelsome beast to cheer up somewhat and the contented one to become aggressive. The conclusion drawn was that new or freshly-distilled whisky *did* have an adverse effect, at least on monkeys, and that its storage to allow maturation appeared to be beneficial.[54] Glasgow firm, Greenlees Brothers, later cashed-in on the tests by bringing out a blend called 'The Monkey Special'. At one point during the same 1890 inquiry a brief reference was made to the notion that an observed increase in lunacy in France was somehow due to fusel-oil-laced spirits!

To some, calling patent-still raw grain spirit 'Real Old Highland Whisky' was in itself an adulteration, as was the use of German spirit in whisky blends that were supposed to be Scottish, but the real problems came about when other starting materials were used instead of malted barley or raw grain in the pot-still process. Potato starch might be added, and this invariably caused an increase in the amount of fusel-oil in the new spirit, more so if more of the feints were included in the final distillate, whether accidentally or intentionally. Such deliberate inclusion of large portions of the feints would have rendered the spirit exceedingly nauseous but would allow a greater volume to be achieved. This would have been unacceptable practise perpetrated by unscrupulous small distillers, both licensed and illicit.

In order to disguise the disgusting taste of fusel-oil, a number of different substances could be added, and these included 'sherry wine, tartaric and acetic acids, sugar, pineapple and other fruit essences, tincture of prunes, acetic ether, oil of wine, spirit of nitrous ether, glycerine, green tea', and others. A common method of converting new whisky into old involved the addition of a mixture of burnt sugar, sherry, acetic ether, and tartaric acid. Many of these were used in such small proportions that they were probably of little risk to the drinker's health, although the fact that they masked the taste of fusel-oil meant the public was exposed unknowingly to a potential poison.[55] The same things might have been added to patent-still whisky to impart colour and taste and give the impression of a 'proper' whisky. Prune wine was in use from around the 1850s as an agent for mellowing spirits, and was said to have exercised a very important influence on the whisky trade.

PATENT PRUNE WINE
Is used by Distillers, Rectifiers, and Wine and Spirit Merchants in all parts of the World, for Fining, Colouring, Purifying, and Mellowing every description of Spirits, including Brandy, Whisky, Rum, and Gin, and renders them more Palatable, more Saleable, and more Wholesome.

The action of Prune Wine upon young Spirits which have often to be put into early consumption to meet the requirements of price, is to neutralise their acrid, fiery, and impure properties, as well as to give the appearance, and in a great measure the qualities of Age – for this purpose it is universally used.[56]

Such a well-used accessory was not regarded as an adulterant but was nevertheless publicly shunned by some. In the 1870s Messrs John Haig & Co of the Cameron Bridge Distillery said, 'We have nothing to do with 'prune wine', 'essence of sherry', or 'Hamburg sherry.' We call our whisky simply 'old still', or 'pot still' whisky, which it undoubtedly is.'[57]

Bad whisky, or that somehow spoiled in the making either through the use of damaged grain, overheating, or the inclusion of noxious parts of the distillate, was almost certainly sold by a few distillers. Once in the hands of the retailer it became even worse, with the usual water dilution followed by the addition of 'Grains of Paradise', capsicum, or whatever.[58] It was the lower classes who suffered most at the hands of publicans, and such were the desperate social conditions in which they were inextricably bound that many were glad to find respite in the contents of a glass. At times it didn't matter if what they were drinking was not whisky, even although it was sold by that name – the title giving an air of normality to an otherwise pathetic scene – and many ended up downing toxic chemical concoctions which only made life worse.

I returned to Glasgow by the railway, and felt my head rather giddy when I got to the station. When going down the High Street, I stepped into —'s spirit cellar in Stirling Street, and paid five *bawbees* for half a gill o' the best whisky. The first thing I recollected after drinking that half-gill of burning stuff – dear knows what was in it – was awaking in the police-office charged with the theft for which I have been convicted.[59]

Bad whisky and crime seemed to go hand in hand.

Very little was heard about the true state of whisky adulteration in Scotland in the mid-nineteenth century. Perhaps the powers that be did not wish to probe too deeply into the spirit that had put Scotland firmly on the world's map for fear of uncovering what the man in the street already knew; the country's reputation could be at risk. The Government was really only beginning to address the problems relating to food and drink, and while it had the 1855 Inquiry and the 1860 Act under its belt and was seen to be doing something, the ineffectual nature of the latter meant that adulteration was still rife.

Whiskey in Ireland was a different matter entirely and numerous cases of its debasement were brought to light. According to the Inland Revenue Report for the year ending 31st March 1872, a gradual change was taking place in the public's taste in spirits. Whereas the English had partaken of their pleasure largely in the form of gin, and those north of the border tended to whet their appetite more with malt whisky, there now appeared to be an inclination towards a spirit 'resembling, and called, Irish whiskey, although certainly not made exclusively in Ireland....'[60] A lot more seemed to be happening across the water and the spirit occupied an ever-increasingly prominent place in the headlines of the day. In 1872 there were eight illicit distillation detections made by the Excise in Scotland. In England there were twenty-one. In Ireland there were one-thousand-one-hundred-and-fifteen! There were reports of sulphuric acid in whisky, as well as 'Methylated Whisky' containing naphtha, cayenne pepper, and other illegal ingredients. Ireland was showing the way with regard to the exposure of spirituous malpractises.

All over the world moves were being made to tackle adulteration. In Poland the addition of lead acetate, small shot, or any other improper substance to wine brought a fine of 10 to 200 roubles or a short term in jail. Anyone convicted of falsifying their wares in Denmark was liable to be fined, while in Norway the crime was punished by imprisonment with a bread and water diet for up to thirty days, or with hard labour for up to three years. In America the Act of the Legislature of the State of New York, passed on April 5th 1870, stated, amongst other things, that 'No distiller or brewer shall manufacture or offer for sale any liquid intended for the drink of human beings which shall be injurious to life or health.' Legislation was in force in New Orleans, but it was felt that no notice was ever taken of liquor adulteration even although it was known to be 'mixed with poisonous materials to a frightful degree, sufficiently expressed by the names of certain beverages, as familiar to the drinkers as damnatory to the drink. 'Rot-gut', 'rifle whisky', 'kill at sixty yards,' are telling epothets, and do not require explanation; yet the law which provides for their prevention is a perfect dead letter.'[61]

The situation in Scotland, and Great Britain, was not much different. It was generally known that whisky was mixed with all manner of toxic ingredients, yet little seemed to be written or done about it. Perhaps the unspoken view of the authorities was that the poorer classes should be left to themselves, at least where alcohol was concerned, and that as long as their problems didn't seep into the cosy world of the middle classes, a blind eye should be turned.

Sadly, the problem was much more serious than anyone could have imagined, and it took the courage of a Glasgow newspaper editor and a young doctor employed at Glasgow University to bring matters to a head. The authorities now *had* to take notice.

The year was 1872.

3

The Mystery Unfolds

IN 1872 in Glasgow 20,144 people were born, 5,121 were married, and 14,047 died. There were around half-a-million people living within the eight square mile area bordered by the parliamentary and municipal boundary, and the inhabitants were said to be more closely housed than in any other city in the United Kingdom.[1] Such cramped and insanitary conditions provided an ideal breeding ground for disease, prostitution, illicit spirit-shops, and crime in every shape and form. Something had to be done. The city fathers were in the process of tackling the problem, and whole streets, along with their dingy closes and alleys, were being wiped off the face of the earth to make way for more modern and spacious structures. Improvements were taking place in the Gallowgate, Bridgegate, Ingram Street, and in South Albion Street where aged and infirm tenements near the City Hall were being unceremoniously razed to ground level. Some of these ancient buildings were in great danger of falling down of their own accord – it might only take an over-zealous party celebration to start timbers creaking ominously and walls bulging dangerously, and before you knew what was happening the whole lot was dingin' doon aroond yer ears.

Should the man in the street have the misfortune to witness his favourite watering-hole being carted away in bits, there was plenty to keep his mind otherwise engaged. Rumours were circulating that a comet was due to hit the earth and inflict calamitous damage on August 12th of that year. Thankfully the story was just a lot of nonsense, but it must nevertheless have driven many to drink a bit more than normal.

Newspapers carried reports of an attempted assassination at Buckingham Palace on Thursday, 29th February, in which a youth presented a pistol (which was not capable of being fired, as it later emerged) at the Queen. Her personal attendant, Brown, apprehended the lad and saved the day.

For those Glaswegians who were a bit bored with it all and needed something to take their mind off the fact that the world might be coming to an end, a trip to Hengler's Cirque, in West Nile Street, would have worked wonders. There they could witness the 'clever exhibition of automatons' performing under the delightful title of Springthorpe's Wondrous Mechanical Little Folks.

However, all was not well beneath the surface, and the first seed of discontent may well have been sown by this letter which appeared in the *Glasgow Herald* on the 25th January:

> Sir – I take the liberty of sending you a few remarks in regard to our national drink – whisky – in the hope that you will be kind enough to insert them in the *Herald* at your convenience.
>
> I, for one, think it strange that the people of Scotland should tamely submit to have their whisky so exorbitantly taxed. That, almost everyone knows, the present high duty paid on our national beverage is not only an inducement to illicit distillation, but the price of good whisky – the most wholesome of drink – being raised to so high a figure, that poor, working men, not being able to purchase the genuine article, are, as it were, compelled to drink nasty, cheap stuff, mixed too often with deleterious drugs, which no doubt, send annually numbers of them to their graves. ...

Adulteration was once more thrust into the limelight in February with the introduction of a new bill in the House of Commons. It is debatable whether any prosecutions had ever been brought under the quite useless 1860 Act and it was felt that the improved legislation would herald a new era in food and drink safety. Unfortunately once the Act came into force, it was also found to be flawed. Prosecutions *were* successfully achieved, but ways were soon found around the wording in the clauses and retailers, in some areas, basked in the knowledge that their essentially illicit practises were not in fact breaking the law. Display of a simple showcard bearing the wording, 'All goods sold here are mixtures and compounds, and no articles will be guaranteed to be genuine,' allowed the retailer to do as he wished.[2] One important improvement in the 1872 Act to Amend the Law for the Prevention of Adulteration of Food and Drink and of Drugs, as it was called, was to compel local authorities to appoint a public analyst. Previously the analysis of food and drink had been undertaken either by the Excise, in the case of duty-bearing goods, or private individuals

Glasgow's High Street, as it looked in 1868, four years before the scandalous state of the city's whisky was exposed. (*Annan Collection, Mitchell Library*).

or organisations who sought to protect the public from all manner of evil.

The Bill which preceded The Licensing Act was also presented to the House of Commons in February, and although dealing with beer and other alcoholic beverages, did put forward a number of clauses which addressed the adulteration crisis. Samples of intoxicating liquor could be taken from premises and analysed. 'Adulteration' and 'analysis' were on the tip of everyone's lips.

The situation in Ireland was also starting to hot up somewhat. Around March or April, two men had found themselves totally incapacitated after drinking a small portion of 'whiskey' which they had purchased in a public house. Once recovered, they took what was left to a Doctor Hodges who, after analysis, found that it contained a large amount of naphtha. Doctor Hodges had carried out tests on other whisky samples in Belfast and discovered copper sulphate, cayenne pepper, sulphuric acid, and other adulterants. One was almost exclusively naphtha coloured with whisky and was said to be 'a fair specimen of the drink sold in low-class public houses.'[3] The spirit had been tampered with after it left the wholesale dealer, no doubt by the publican, and distillers and spirit dealers were up in arms to ensure that their reputation had not been tarnished. No prosecutions took place, and it was felt that it was in *everyone's* interest to ensure that a stop was put to such practises. The public airing would have gone some way towards achieving this.

In April, part of the evidence heard by the Select Committee of the House of Commons, which was inquiring into the best method of treating habitual drunkards, came from Doctor McGill, a surgeon who had been with the police-force in Glasgow for sixteen years. He referred to a report by the city's Chief Constable, Mr McCall, in which he said, 'Drink was oftentimes sold when largely and perniciously adulterated. So strong was the craving for drink, that men would take naphtha or any kind of stimulant.'[4] This was certainly true of Ireland where ether was used as an intoxicant in some areas, and was taken in preference to whiskey to such an extent that it was in danger of becoming the new national drink![5] Of course the situation in Glasgow was nowhere near as bad as that in Ireland – or was it?

Secret Meetings
Doctor Charles Cameron was editor of the *North British Daily Mail*. He

started life on a completely different path and became a Graduate in Medicine before making a special study of practical and inorganic chemistry. At university he carried out many analytical tests on spirits, the experience standing him in good stead for the lengthy quest which lay before him. His thirst for knowledge did not abate and he then went on to take his 'Bachelor of Arts Degree as First of the First Honour Men, and Gold Medalist in Experimental and Natural Sciences.' Cameron was much more than an editor.

There can be little doubt that while sitting at his desk in the late summer of 1872 many things were going through his mind. There was a newspaper to take care of, and while it was important to bring recent events, at home and abroad, to his readers attention, it was equally important to be continually seeking new topics and angles; big stories didn't always happen of their own accord – they sometimes needed a bit of prompting. Being gifted with a sense of fair play, there was always some wrong that could be put right by public exposure in his broadsheet.

Cameron could not have spent so much time at university without retaining an interest in the subjects he had studied, and it is highly likely that while working as an editor his reading material would have included a fair selection of medical and chemical journals. He would be keen to learn of recent research developments and perhaps even missed the practical and theoretical side of his previous scholarly life. Had he been a reader of the *British Medical Journal,* he would have been aware of the gross adulteration of whisky in Belfast, and this must have struck a very deep chord. Thoughts of previous letters and reports on the dreadful state of Scotland's national drink would have remained locked in a prominent position in his mind, occasionally being unleashed and toyed with along with memories of his own analytical tests on spirits.

On August 10th the improved adulteration Act entered the statute-books, and by this date Cameron almost certainly had a rough idea of what his next big story was. And what a story. He would take samples of whisky from some of the rougher public houses in Glasgow and have them analysed. If the results were as he anticipated, and all the signs indicated that this would be the case, another scandal would have been exposed. There had only been occasional rumours about the condition of Glasgow's whisky up to this point in time, and none of them proved, but with conclusive evidence in black and white the authorities could no longer turn a blind eye – they would have to take action.

While putting his thoughts into a practical formula, he read the August edition of the *Glasgow Medical Journal* and could not help but notice a review which gave great credit to the author of a work which examined the chemistry and detection of the poison strychnine. Praise was given for the original research and chemical studies executed in the laboratory, and while there were one or two niggly criticisms regarding typographical errors, on the whole it was well-received. The author was young, full of energy and ability, and showed immense promise for producing even better work. His name was Doctor James St. Clair Gray.

James St. Clair Gray was born in Perth in 1847. He was the eldest son of physician James Gray and his wife Mary Sinclair, his brothers and sisters numbering eight. Around 1852 the family moved to Glasgow and lived for a while in a flat at 1 Newton Street, while James the elder set up in practice at 305 Sauchiehall Street. Several years later they moved to a house at 8 Newton Street, but business on the medical front was obviously booming because around 1861 they moved again to the newly-constructed and very fashionable Newton Terrace, at number fifteen. It is generally thought that this terrace was built c1864-5, but Glasgow's Post Office Directory clearly mentions numbers 1 to 3 in 1859/60, construction obviously under way but not complete, and the whole section of numbers 1 to 18 is listed in 1860/61. The census of 1861 mentions them as staying at this address, an eleven-roomed house, along with three servants.

In 1869 James St. Clair Gray graduated into the world of medicine at Glasgow University, and in 1871 became a Doctor of Medicine. The university was then moving lock, stock, and barrel from its Old College site in the High Street to Gilmorehill, beside Gilmorehill House, and he must have studied at both locations. Between 1869 and 1872 he was Assistant to Harry Rainy, the Professor of Medical Jurisprudence at Glasgow University, an eminent gentleman who had occupied that chair for upwards of thirty years, between 1841 and 1872. On Rainy's retiral the *Glasgow Medical Journal* had this to say: 'No man could leave his class-room without having benefited by contact with his pre-eminently logical mind, and by the example of his cautious, precise method of investigation.' Although his assistant for only about three

The Faculty of Physicians and Surgeons of Glasgow, c1870. Among the many eminent medical men of the period, this composite photograph features:
1. Doctor James St. Clair Gray.
2. Doctor James Gray, father of the above.
3. Professor Harry Rainy, to whom Doctor James St. Clair Gray was assistant between 1869 and 1872.
(*The Royal College of Physicians and Surgeons of Glasgow*).

years, Gray would undoubtedly have learned a great deal from such a well-respected man. The nature of Rainy's work meant that Gray received much experience of poisons and toxins and would have been familiar and well-versed in the use of analytical methods for their detection. The *Glasgow Medical Journal* during this period reported much of the work with which he was involved.

On the 4th of November 1870, at a meeting of the Medico-Chirurgical Society, Gray exhibited a 'modification of Marsh's Apparatus,' used for detecting arsenic and antimony. Also on the forensic side, on the 20th of January 1871, at a meeting of the same society, he read a paper titled 'An Analysis of 143 Cases of Poisoning with Strychnia,' which included details of Gray seeking 'absolutely conclusive evidence' when detecting the poison in body tissues or fluids.[6] In August of that year Gray had an original article published in the *Glasgow Medical Journal* titled 'Two Cases of Poisoning by Aconite' (otherwise known as wolf's-bane, a deadly poison), in which he detailed instances witnessed while on rounds with his father. One of these involved the accidental administration of the poison by a wet-nurse to a child. Death by poisoning was a common occurance in those days, poor lighting and indistinct bottles and labels being frequently blamed by virtue of their making it difficult to identify the contents and required dosage. The ease of access to poisons and the criminal intent of some was also to blame, and the Government was clamping down by extending their control and restricting their availability. The Pharmacy Act of 1868 stated, amongst other things, that the word 'Poison' must appear on the label, but clearly in the dimness of gas lighting this measure would have had little impact.

In November of the same year, Gray read a paper to the Medico-Chirurgical Society on 'Animal Electricity and its Relations to the Functions of the Animal Economy.' His interests within the medical field were diverse, but his main work was with poisons, and to this he returned in the summer of 1872 with his first book – *Strychnia: Its Source, Chemical Relations, Physiological Action (Typical and Irregular), Mode of Detection, and Methods of Treatment in Cases of Poisoning*. The title pretty much indicates what the content is. Such was the degree of precision with which the analytical tests were conducted that Gray was able to say, with regard to the detection of strychnine, 'I should be declined to limit the delicacy of the test to the two hundred and fifty thousandth of a grain ....'

Doctor James St. Clair Gray, as taken from the composite photograph, c1870.

This might all seem very far removed from whisky, mysteries, and the like, but in charting Gray's scholarly career – and remember, he was young; only twenty-four when the whisky tests were conducted – I think it will now be obvious that he was a man who was dedicated to his work, very capable of detecting minute traces of substances by analytical methods, and clearly destined for great things. He was indeed one of a number of candidates who were considered for the chair vacated by Professor Rainy's retiral.[7] Doctor Cameron, the *'Mail's* editor, had found the right analyst for the job.

Before continuing, let's spend a brief moment looking at the other options open to Doctor Cameron. The Excise laboratory in London was too far away and, besides, while wanting to expose criminal activity, Cameron did not wish to provide evidence upon which publicans could be prosecuted. The Excise would want to follow through with such action and was therefore not suitable for the analytical task that lay ahead. Of course they probably would not have wanted to be involved anyway. If gross adulteration was discovered, it would reflect badly on their ability to keep the problem in check, as was their responsibility. No, the names of the public houses had to remain a secret; nothing could be gained from revealing their identity, not to mention the large number of enemies that might be made by divulging such potentially widespread fraud and naming the perpetrators!

The most obvious choice for the analyst was probably Robert R. Tatlock of the firm Wallace, Tatlock & Clark, based in the analytical laboratory at 42 Bath Street, Glasgow. At the time of Cameron's whisky analysis all three directors of this company were on the verge of becoming public analysts for the city of Glasgow, and such was their position that, like the Excise, prosecutions would have to follow. Tatlock would not be suitable either.

Although attached to the university, Gray was, in essence, a private individual whose only task was to analyse the samples given to him. He had no interest in ensuring that the powers of the law were brought to bear upon those who might tamper with spirits, and for this reason Cameron saw in him the perfect choice. Perhaps he also saw in him that same youthful drive and energy that he himself had exhibited during his earlier studious days. Here was a young man who showed great promise and who might well move on to truly great things – Cameron was giving him a helping hand along the way.

But did Cameron think Gray the right man for the job for the right reasons? Might he not have taken advantage of such youthful and inexperienced enthusiasm? Might he have prompted him with views on what the samples might contain, and might Gray have found what he was expected to find, and not what his results indicated? There is absolutely no reason to suppose that this was the case. The type of work which Gray was involved with at the university would ensure that *everything* he tackled in the laboratory would be given the same degree of intensive scrutiny to which he was accustomed. The reason I have introduced this sceptical intrusion is because, as we shall see later, a number of more mature and experienced scientists were to voice serious concern over the manner in which the analytical tests were undertaken and sought to prove that Gray could not have achieved the results he did. My own personal opinion is that Gray was a far greater scientist than any of them realised, but sadly he was not given the chance to prove it.

It is not known exactly when the samples were collected, or indeed how they were collected, but the '*Mail* gives us one or two clues with which to piece together the possible sequence of events. On looking at the date of publication of the first set of results, and assuming an approximate timescale of about one week to analyse all thirty samples,

The Gray family home at 15 Newton Terrace, Glasgow, as it looks today. (*Edward Burns*).

then Gray must have received them around the beginning of September. Cameron read Gray's book review in August, so they probably met for the first time (if they didn't already know each other) in the second half of that month when Cameron would have requested Gray's assistance and ascertained the volume of whisky needed to carry out the tests. Both men would have been excited by the venture, but, although having a rough idea of what they were letting themselves in for, could not possibly have envisaged the furore that was to follow.

The samples *may* have been taken by Cameron, as suggested in the fictional reconstruction in Chapter One, but this is unlikely. He would have looked and sounded far too respectable to be seen drinking in the type of place due to be visited, and publicans, suspecting him of being an Excise Officer or some other figure of authority, would have served him the 'good' whisky as opposed to the stuff usually sold to their regular customers. For this reason, a second, suitably-attired party would have been despatched to discretely collect the samples, probably with a witness.

In the case of the unlicensed public houses, or shebeens, it would have been far too dangerous for any person not known to the owner to enter the premises and furtively leave with some whisky, albeit paid for, hidden on their person. Respectable shebeens were known to exist, but certainly not in the city centre areas around the Saltmarket, High Street, and in the closes and wynds leading off from the Trongate where the bulk of the samples would have been collected. These samples were therefore provided by police officers, either through the results of a raid or via paid informers who were known to frequent the premises in question.

It is conceivable that Cameron had previous knowledge of particular public houses, either through discussions with police officers, colleagues, or through the public grapevine, and knew which were the most likely to yield the worst and most spectacular results. This would ensure that the story, once published, had a much greater impact than if only one or two cases of adulteration were discovered. Even if this was true, and there is nothing to suggest that it was, the implications would be the same in that some of Glasgow's public houses had a serious adulteration problem.

The Mysteries of Glasgow Whisky
On the 25th of September 1872, the story broke.

The results of fifteen samples were given initially, and the following is a transcript of the first few paragraphs which opened the whole shebang, as presented to the public in the pages of the *North British Daily Mail*:

THE MYSTERIES OF GLASGOW WHISKY

We believe that topers and teetotalers will alike agree with the sagacious remark of the traditional Highlandman – "It's a bad thing whisky, especially bad whisky" – and in the present investigation we would wish it to be particularly understood that it is against *bad* whisky we wage a war. The results of excess in the unadulterated article are lamentable enough, but when it comes to the drinking of methylated spirit, wood naphtha, and "finish", under the guise of "guid Scots drink," whereby the Excise is cheated, and the consumer is poisoned a good deal more quickly that he bargains for, it is time that the authorities should interfere. And in our investigations into the nature of the so-called whiskies sold in Glasgow, so far as the specimens obtained from public-houses are concerned, although we had sixteen different samples, procured in widely distant quarters of the city, analysed, we are sorry to say we failed to find among them a single example of the genuine unsophisticated article. Luckily for the safety of the drinking public, the adulterators seem to have a strong partiality for Loch Katrine water, and whatever condiments they may employ to impart a flavour to that rather insipid fluid, they, as a rule, prefer to sell their "whisky" in the form of grog. Otherwise the death-rate of the city would probably be a good deal larger than it is. Of course, we do not mean to say that there are not in Glasgow many respectable publicans who honestly dispense pure liquor; but the extent of the nefarious competition to which they are subjected may be inferred from the fact that in 16 public houses in various parts of the city – mostly, it is but fair to state, second and third rate concerns – from which we procured samples for examination, in not one instance did we find a specimen free from adulteration. We abstain from publishing the names of the parties by whom the liquor was sold, for to gibbet a few men for an iniquity to which they are probably no more addicted than hundreds of others could serve no good purpose. Moreover, our business is not to act as detectives, but simply to expose a system in which there can be little doubt a large proportion of the intoxication and crime of the city originate.

Before considering individual specimens it may be well shortly to glance at the adulterants more commonly employed. Those which are of all others the impurities most frequently found are water, wood naphtha or methylic alcohol, and potato spirits, otherwise known as fousel oil or amylic alcohol. We may explain that although in popular parlance there is but one alcohol, scientifically speaking, there is a series composed of the same elements, but arranged in different proportions. Of these the alcohol with which were are familiar in brandy, whisky, beer, etc., is ethylic. That which is termed methylic is of a taste so repulsive that spirits mixed with a certain percentage of it are allowed to pass untaxed by the Excise, it being supposed that they are thereby unfitted for drinking purposes. As to amylic alcohol, which is a prominent constituent of potato spirit, it is untaxed, and employed largely in arts and manufactures and chemical processes. It may perhaps here be necessary to state that while wood naphtha should never by any chance exist in whisky taken from the still, yet it is not uncommon to find amylic alcohol in those which have been low run – by which expression is meant that the temperature has been so raised as to force over in the distillate materials which are incapable of distillation at the temperature ordinarily required for the volatilisation of whisky. This is principally due to the fact that the distiller is required to produce from a given quantity of material subjected to distillation a certain proportion of whisky, so that the incentive is very strong thus to force from less productive materials the average proportion of spirit. This, then, is a fault which requires correction, and this must be looked for entirely at the hands of the revenue officials. Next to these, we have as adulterants oil of vitriol or sulphuric acid, turpentine, sulphate of zinc, sulphate of copper, chloride of sodium or common salt, shellac, chlorine water, caramel or burnt sugar, commonly known as rum colouring, saccharine, gummy, and extractive matters, and, in a few instances, wines of very low quality, as prune wine, to which many whiskies owe their rich dark yellow tinge. In this list also might be included the addition of Canadian maize whisky and French brandies of low quality. These, then, are the most commonly used adulterants, but as nearly every mixer of whisky has his own particular formula, it may be reasonably inferred that this list, large as it is, is not complete. It is, however, so far a complete enumeration of those substances fraudulently admixed in the whiskies which have in the course of the present examination been submitted to analysis, and we trust sufficiently full to show to those interested in the subject the manner in which the public are swindled, and the revenue defrauded.

The actual results were then given, and although the 'Mail had offered some explanation with regard to the facts and figures that followed, it all must have looked pretty complicated to the man in the street. The first result was as follows:

No. 1
Public-house Islay Whisky

Colour – Pale straw.

Taste – Harsh disagreeable alcoholic (methylic and amylic struggling for pre-eminence; ethylic completely masked).

Strength – 22.8 per cent under proof.

Reaction – Acid to test paper.

No hydrochloric acid, and no soluble chloride present.

Sulphuric acid, free and combined as sulphate of zinc – 40 grs. per gallon.

Ethylic, methylic, and amylic alcohols, of specific gravity .820 – About 70 ounces per gallon.

Turpentine – Decided traces.

Gummy, saccharine, and resinous matters – 180 grs. per gallon.

Water – Rather beyond 90 ounces per gallon.

   Note – The proportion of methylic alcohol in this specimen was such that the ethylic alcohol must have been in great part, if not entirely derived from methylated spirits, the fousel oil and turpentine being apparently added with a view to disguise the smell of the methyl, as well as to increase the intoxicating effect, and to render the taste more pungent. It is possible that the fousel oil above referred to might have been derived from very low run spirit.

Although the figures might appear a bit confusing to the layman, it doesn't take a professor to see that something is sadly amiss, and in anyone's books turpentine and methylated spirits do not combine in some magical way to form whisky of any sort. The rest of the results were not much better. Little will be gained at this moment in time by the reproduction of all tests carried out, as outlined in No. 1 above, but I feel it will be of some interest to give the notes which accompanied each one. Numbers 1 to 14 were public house whiskies, and No. 15 was a shebeen whisky.

   No.2 – In this specimen whisky was decidedly present, but in addition thereto, fousel oil in considerable proportions, derived apparently from low run whisky, as well as methylic alcohol, probably as methylated spirits, the object being to increase the quantity of saleable spirits.

   No. 3 – Evidently a mixture of wood spirits with whisky, or else a very low run whisky, with a considerable proportion of water.

No. 4 – Consists principally of low run whisky with very considerable quantities of fousel oil, Berlin spirits and turpentine added thereto.

No. 5 – Evidently a mixture of low run whisky with Berlin spirit; water in excess.

No. 6 – A combination in the main of very low run raw grain spirits with methylated spirits; appears to have been treated with charcoal, probably to destroy to a certain extent the smell, as well as to remove excess of colouring matter. Water in excess.

No. 7 – Evidently a mixture of impure methylated spirits with low run whisky, the other substances being added with a view to disguise the smell, and at the same time to increase the biting properties of the article. Water much in excess of the correct proportion.

No. 8 – A fair sample of medium whisky – probably a blend of raw grain spirits with low run malt whisky.

No. 9 – This specimen evidently owes its peculiar smell and taste to a considerable extent to the presence of apple brandy. Water in excessive quantity presence.

No. 10 – The presence here of sulphuric ether is probably to be accounted for by the action of free sulphuric acid in the alcohol. Water present in great excess.

No. 11 – The peculiar metallic·taste evidently due to the presence of copper as a soluble salt in the sample. The alcohol present consists partly of raw grain spirit, partly of very low run malt whisky, and partly of methylated spirit.

No. 12 – A fair specimen of whisky, but water added to too great an extent.

No. 13 – A good whisky, free from adulteration, save with water, of which the proportion is too great.

No. 14 – A good whisky, free from adulteration, save with water.

No. 15 – Probably contains no pure whisky, as the proportion of Berlin spirit and methylated spirit, as well as Fousel oil, is such as to preclude the presence of more than an ounce or two of the genuine spirit in each gallon. Water in excessive proportion.

The second set of results was published on the 30th of September, and in the short five-day gap between the two dates, eight letters appeared in the 'Mail's pages. 'Thank God I am a teetotaler,' came the statement from one 'shocked' reader, while another, writing under the nom de plume 'Touch Not', wrote – 'It is impossible to tell of the fearful havoc that those compounds may have wrought, of the numberless graves they may have filled, the low, sad wails of agony they may have caused to ascend from the broken hearts of the orphan and the widow, of the bodies consigned to untimely graves, of the souls they may have hurried into an unprepared-for eternity.'[8]

Not all letters were just as poetic as that above. Fears were voiced over whether it was safe to drink in *any* of the public houses in Glasgow, and lovers of a wee drappie o't became quite rightly concerned and perhaps even a little frightened. Calls were made for the '*Mail*' to reveal the names of the vendors of this so-called 'whisky' so that honest traders could be allowed to sell their wares without being eyed suspiciously by the public.

No one was more concerned than the Glasgow Wine, Spirit, and Beer Trade Association who, following the '*Mail's* report, must have been having proverbial kittens. The Secretary, William Smyth, immediately penned a letter in which he said that 'few, if any, persons in the trade in Scotland would knowingly adulterate drink.' When one considers the extent of adulteration all over the world during this period, it is hard to believe that Scotland would be any different. The Glasgow Wine, Spirit, and Beer Trade Association must have been living in cloud-cuckoo-land. Of course, they probably had a fair idea that some adulteration went on, but they couldn't be seen to admit to such knowledge lest their good name should fall into disrepute. The real problem, as far as they were concerned, was that the '*Mail's* report indicated that practically *every* public house in Glasgow was at it.

Mr Smyth's letter then became quite abusive towards the '*Mail*. He accused them of producing a one-sided article which was typical of the sensational character periodically indulged in by the paper, and went on to say that the public were the 'best judges of what suits them, and will not form an unfavourable opinion of the whole trade merely for the alleged and unproved delinquencies of a few.' This was fighting talk. Cameron had to respond:

> Had the members of the Glasgow Wine, Spirit, and Beer Trade read the introduction to our report they would have seen that we were careful to state that we waged war not against whisky, but against *bad* whisky. We also expressed our belief in the existence of honest publicans, who also would hail with satisfaction the suppression of the iniquitous traffic we exposed. We only said that, having had sixteen specimens of public house whisky procured in various parts of the city analysed, we did not find one which was not more or less adulterated, and we are prepared to substantiate the statement on oath. ....

Cameron then went on to say that not one of the 'Mail's previous exposures – the Truck Commission, the Sanitary Commission, or its Baby-Farming Commission – had ever been proved inaccurate or untrue. He finished on an equally scathing attack on the Association's apparent inability to manage its own house and keep its members from fraudulently tampering with the good name of Scotland's national drink.

One or two letters were quite technical and demonstrated a certain knowledge of distillation, spirits, and chemistry. One reader, known simply as 'W' (for Wallace?), commented on low run whisky and feints, and said that the amount of amylic alcohol or fousel oil which should be left in spirits was a point on which no two distillers could agree – 'and that in some of the very finest whiskies the amount of feints is so large as to give a colour to the spirit, and also a disagreeable smell when new; yet, when this spirit is matured by age and the lees of wine, it possesses such a rich flavour as to command a very high price in the market.' According to 'W', if such a spirit had fallen into the hands of an inexperienced chemist for analysis when new, 'it might probably be marked as containing decided traces of turpentine, and that the amylic and methylic alcohols were so abundant as to mask the presence of the ethylic alcohol.'

Doctor Gray must have read each day's paper with some interest. Day by day would come the slow realisation that this was one analytical excursion that couldn't be done and forgotten about. Questions were being asked. Had he detected turpentine and methyl alcohol, or was it as 'W' had suggested, a simple case of a new whisky with a large proportion of feints?

Meanwhile, on the 30th of September the second set of results were published. The 'Mail opened with a defence against some of the criticisms that had come its way over the previous few days. Fusel (or Fousel)-oil, while of course being present in new whisky, was in fact used as an adulterant by the dishonest retailer. It was apparently duty-free, and could be purchased for around 1s-6d to 2s per gallon as opposed to 14s for the cheapest whisky, 10s of which was duty.

> To give an idea of the extent to which the nefarious use of this substance
> is carried out in our midst, we may mention that we are informed, on
> reliable authority, that a single commission agent in this city in a single
> month disposed of 10,000 gallons of fousel oil through channels which

Doctor Charles Cameron, Editor of the *North British Daily Mail*, as depicted in *The Bailie* in October 1873, with whisky samples No. 9, 16 and 17 standing conspicuously beside him. (*Mitchell Library*).

left little doubt that the greater portion, if not the whole of it, was intended to be employed in the adulteration of whisky.[9]

The 'Mail then backed up the finding of methyl alcohol in some of the samples by saying that, unlike amyl alcohol, it should never find its way into whisky unless introduced with fraudulent intent. Methylated spirits could be bought for 3s-6d to 6s per gallon, and was untaxed so as to allow its use in various industries. While it had ten per cent methyl alcohol to ninety of ethyl so as to make it quite unpalatable, its low cost must have been a great inducement to use it as a beverage, the obnoxious taste being made bearable by the addition of various substances like sherry wine and fruit essences, in much the same way as the taste of fusel-oil could be disguised.

A certain amount of confusion or misunderstanding was then displayed by the 'Mail, and centred around the definition of the word 'finish', a name given to a weak varnish made from methylated spirits and shellac gum. Berlin spirit, according to the 'Mail, was also termed 'finish' when it had shellac added. This seems to go against all post-1855 definitions (the date when methylated spirits was first prepared and used in industry), although there is every reason to suppose that prior to 1855 other alcohols were used with shellac to form a varnish which, in being used to finish off an item of furniture or the exterior of a hat, was simply termed 'finish'. This apparent mix-up was later used as ammunition by those who failed to believe the validity of the whisky analysis and sought to denigrate Doctor Gray's name. However, no matter how much nit-picking was done by the sceptics in attempting to belittle the whole analysis, there was no getting away from the finding of methyl alcohol and shellac – some of the whisky *had* contained 'finish', and the exact definition of the word was of little consequence. It was, nevertheless, one of a number of sticking-points over which much discussion would follow.

In concluding the preamble before the second set of data, the 'Mail mentioned the recently passed Act to Amend the Law for the Prevention of Adulteration of Food and Drink and of Drugs, and called for a public analyst to be appointed at once to enforce the Act.

Moreover, any person selling any article of food or drink mixed with any other substance with intent fraudulently to increase its weight or bulk, without declaring the mixture at the time of sale, shall be deemed to have sold an adulterated article under the Act.

The appointment of a public analyst was essential in aiding the implementation of this Act, and the 'Mail's whisky scandal exposé merely highlighted the necessity that this position be filled as swiftly as possible.

Of the second fifteen results, No. 16 was a public house Irish whiskey, No. 28 was a public house whisky, and Nos. 29 and 30 were purchased as high-class whiskies, the latter Irish, from wine merchants. All the rest were shebeen samples. As before, only the notes will be quoted at present, that is, with the exception of No. 27, which is of some interest.

No. 16 – This is probably a mixture of low run whisky, with inferior brandy, the colour being heightened by the addition of large quantities of caramel, that is, burnt sugar commonly known as rum colouring.

No. 17 – Evidently the amount of whisky present in this sample is extremely small, the bulk of spirit consisting of methylated spirit, Berlin spirit, and very low run spirit, commonly called feints. Water present to an excessive degree.

No. 18 – Consists principally of low run whisky watered, the other ingredients being added to increase the bite.

No. 19 – The principal ingredient of this so-called whisky is water, to which are added Berlin spirit, potato spirit, methylated spirit, sulphate of copper, and turpentine, to give to the resulting compound an odour and taste in some degree resembling whisky.

No. 20 – Remarks applied to specimen No. 19 may be applied here.

No. 21 – No whisky present. The basis of operation here is Berlin spirit, to which, in the first instance, water is added, the other ingredients being added, probably with a view to suit the tastes of the customers who patronise such beverages.

No. 22, 23, 24 – (practically identical) – All prepared by mixing a large quantity of Berlin spirit with water, adding a small quantity of low run spirit, and working up to increase the bite by the addition of the other ingredients mentioned. (Crude acetic acid, turpentine, etc.)

No. 25 – Consists entirely of Berlin spirit, wood naphtha, and a small quantity of very low class whisky and a few extraneous matters tending to increase the bite, with water in very large proportion.

No. 26 – Contains no whisky. The principal ingredients are Berlin spirit, wood naphtha or methylated spirit, and water. Rest added to increase bite.

No. 27
Shebeen Whisky

Colour – Pinkish green.
Smell – Indescribable.
Taste – Disgusting.
Strength – 41.4 per cent under proof.
Reaction – Neutral.
Sulphuric Acid and Sulphates – Absent.
Hydrochloric Acid and Chlorides – Absent.
Turpentine – Traces.
Shellac – Large quantitie.
Methylic and Ethylic Alcohols of sp. gr. .820 – about 45 oz. per gallon.
Gummy and extractive matters – About 2 per cent.
Water – About 112 oz. per gallon.
   Note – Pure Berlin spirit or finish, reduced by addition of water, is the principal constituent of this sample.

No. 28 – Low run whisky constitutes principal ingredient here reduced with water.
No. 29 – A perfectly pure whisky; colour probably due to caramel.
No. 30 – A very good whisky, but rather new.

Before looking at one or two letters from the deluge that hit the offices of the 'Mail following the above piece, it might be interesting to briefly skirt a few of the issues which immediately spring to mind. First of all, numbers 22, 23, and 24 are practically identical, and this may indicate any one of a number of things. It could mean that all three shebeens obtained their 'whisky' from the same source, which in turn means that the stuff was being made on a fairly large-scale wholesale basis. This is of some importance, as it swiftly vaporises any quaint, but none-the-less horrific, images of crafty individuals haphazardly mixing some of this and some of that in an effort to diddle their customers (who would be unlikely to complain to the authorities as they themselves were taking part in an illicit activity), and brings to mind a certain degree of organisation. Alternatively it could mean that all three shebeens were owned by the same person, and it was he who made the 'blend' to provide to his outlets. Or, it may be three solitary owners all working to the same recipe, perhaps one that was common knowledge, easy and cheap to make, and deemed passable by the drinking fraternity. Either way, it is indicative of the criminal web which pervaded Glasgow's spirituous dens and howffs.

It is also worth mentioning at this stage that the 'Mail appears to have shied away from an explanation regarding the presence of turpentine in some of the samples. Evidence was provided for the use of fusel-oil and for methyl alcohol, but the inclusion of turpentine, while being a great headliner, seems to have been a rather peculiar and unwarranted embarrassment. There is little justification for adding turpentine to whisky, even for the shebeen owner, but then maybe it was a case of adding *anything* to disguise the taste of other adulterants. It was a vicious circle. However, while the 'Mail could find no plausible explanation at the time, there is indeed a number of ways in which the cunning shebeener could introduce turpentine into his 'whisky', not directly, but as a result of adding a liquid in which it was mixed, and we shall look more closely at this in a later chapter.

Experts, Excise, and Councillor Steel

The following letter is, in my view, one of the most important in the whole affair, and comes before all the petty arguments developed over the analysis. As will be seen, everyone *knew* that whisky (along with everything else) was adulterated, but learned men of science need absolute proof before they will believe anything, and as far as many were concerned the analytical proof provided by the 'Mail and Doctor Gray was not enough. In their eyes there was nothing amiss with Glasgow's whisky. How very wrong they were.

> Sir, – Taking as a chemist considerable interest in the discussion originating in your columns concerning the mysteries of Glasgow whisky, I am much astonished at the letter of Mr Smith, secretary to the Glasgow, Wine, Spirit, and Beer Trade Association. It appears to me that this association has laid itself open to censure in so far as it has not been the first to discover and disclose the nefarious practises of which members of the liquor trade are evidently guilty. I hold it specially worthy of notice that for years all practical chemists, particularly those whose services have been required in questions bearing upon adulterations in general, have known that this system of fraud has been extensively practised not only in the whisky trade in the large towns and

villages of Scotland, but also in other parts of the United Kingdom. In fact it is not long since the eyes of the Irish populace were opened regarding the sophistication of Irish whisky, and at that time I believe facts were reported even more astounding than those elicited by your commissioners. From what I have learned personally from various revenue officers, distillers, wholesale and retail vendors of whisky, as well as from consumers, I can infer that to many of them the report published in Wednesday's *Mail* contained little new information, if indeed any. The following is the first of a very recent conversation with two extensive wine merchants: – They both had heard it frequently stated that the constituents referred to in your report might be found in whisky, and that they could understand how the addition of methylated and Berlin spirits should be resorted to with a view to increase the quantity of saleable liquor. Besides they had been informed that sulphuric acid and various sulphates were added to produce the bead, whilst they explained the presence of fousel oil by the addition of low run to pure strong spirit; and the presence of lead, copper, and zinc to impurities received in distillation or subsequent handling of the material. Turpentine, they said, could only enter the whisky from the bung or bung-cloth, which was frequently anointed with turpentine and rosin. After the analysis of the liquor you received it is no longer a mystery how the detected shebeener could invariably afford the heavy penalties imposed for his illicit traffic. ...

I am, etc.,
ESPIRIT DE CORPS.[10]

Other less knowledgeable, but nevertheless equally supportive, letters appeared at the same time, some attacking the Glasgow Wine, Spirit, and Beer Trade Association, and others lamenting the demise of John Barleycorn – murdered by poison!

The *Glasgow Herald* then entered the arena and added weight to the increasing demand that the name of the whisky analyst be revealed to all. His anonymity was regarded with great suspicion by some who felt that the results might be exaggerated, the minor inconsistencies pointing towards a newspaper plot in which a third-rate analyst – or even none at all – was used.

Doctor Cameron, the *'Mail's* editor, must then have had talks with Doctor Gray and, against both their wishes, the latter's name was published. Gray had been assisted in smelling and tasting the samples by experts connected with the spirit trade who were 'thoroughly conversant with most of the forms of adulteration in practice', and the

'Mail assured its readers that its editor did not commit his newspaper to the publication of the articles which had created so much excitement 'without most carefully satisfying himself as to the conscientiousness, accuracy, and ability with which the analyses were performed.'

Then Councillor James Steel put in his tuppence worth. Mr Steel seems to have had an uncanny ability to put his foot in it every time he put pen to paper or opened his mouth. In May of that year he made a speech, as Chairman of the Wine and Spirit Merchants' Benevolent Institution, at a dinner of the Wine and Spirit Trade Association in which he recommended that his brethren in the trade 'drink deep and fill their skins brimful of the nectar of Bass and the sherbet of Allsopp.' To say that this created a bit of a stir would probably be a gross understatement, judging by the numerous letters that hit the press following his verbal gaff. It was, of course, well known that publicans were often faced with temptation, and the last thing they needed was advice to quaff gallons of beer. In the context of excessive drinking, Steel's statement was in bad taste.

So, when Steel submitted his letter to the 'Mail in connection with Glasgow whisky, it was sure to either get someone's back up or give everyone a laugh – or both! He started thus:

> Sir, – I should not think it worth while to notice the watery ebullitions of the new teetotal claquerie; their impudence and forwardness are the results of their ignorance, excited by the profitableness of moral clacking in this country; but when the ministers of the religion of truth and men of science (so they name themselves) fly to the newspapers to have a fling at the poor publican, with no better foundation to stand upon than your general analyses of the whiskies of the city, I think it is time the thing was stopped.[11]

He then mounted an attack on the letter writer Espirit de Corps for not bringing his knowledge of adulteration to the attention of the authorities – 'What sort of conscience must this correspondent have, to rush into print to attack unscientific publicans for not discovering these sophistications and exposing them, while he, a scientific man, knew all about them, and yet neglected his duty to the revenue and to society through these long years of his knowledge ....' In addition, if revenue officers were aware of the various forms of whisky adulteration, as mentioned in Espirit de Corps's letter, why then were there no prosecutions in this area? – 'Are the Excise, like himself, in league with the supposed guilty ones, defrauding the Crown and poisoning the lieges?'

The above two points raised by Councillor Steel might appear, on the surface, rather fair and warranted, but they certainly didn't apply to the real world. The blending and mixing of whiskies was at a very early stage – only a couple of decades old in the 1870s – and a number of extraneous substances were added to help this amalgamation on its way. There was no such thing as a list of substances that could or couldn't be added to whisky subsequent to its distillation. Prune wine might be added to counteract the taste and effect of fusel-oil, as might essence of sherry, but it went without saying that there was only a small number of things that could be employed before whisky ceased to be whisky and became some other peculiar alcoholic cocktail. As far as blending was concerned, who is to say that turpentine wasn't added by some small-time merchant who considered it to be of great benefit to his house 'Special'? It is unlikely that it would have been intentionally added on its own, but I make the point to demonstrate the at times ambiguous nature of the term 'whisky', more so in illicit circles where anything and everything was flung into the 'blending'-pot. Besides, it's really no more absurd than the known addition of glycerine, green tea, and other items, the only difference (and an important one at that) being that the latter are relatively harmless. Where did blending stop and adulteration begin? It was a very complex question.

So, although Espirit de Corps had the knowledge of certain malpractises (along with the rest of the world), the loose and accepted use of blending enhancers, combined with the ineffectiveness of the 1860 Act for Preventing the Adulteration of Articles of Food or Drink, meant that little could be done. The improved 1872 Act had only just come into force and the authorities were still finding their feet with regard to its application.

Councillor Steel's joker was then laid on the table.

> I believe that nearly all the substances noticed by your analyst will be found in a greater or less degree native to whisky – many of them are quite as harmless as alcohol, which seems to be taken by the teetotalers as the emblem of purity.

A typical Victorian public house; the Old Basin Tavern, Baird's Brae, located near the Forth & Clyde Canal at Hamiltonhill, Glasgow. (*Graham Collection, Mitchell Library*).

Here then was evidence that the man had taken leave of his senses, his use of the word 'nearly' doing nothing to lessen the ludicrous impact of his statement. Sulphuric acid, turpentine, methylated spirits, shellac – all native to whisky? Of course, perhaps the councillor was not referring to whisky fresh from the still, and had more knowledge about malpractices in mixing than he was letting on!

It was not long before irate readers flooded the offices of the *'Mail* with letters. 'It is a treat to meet occasionally with one of Councillor Steel's literary efforts – if not very instructive, they are at least very amusing,' wrote one James MacNair. An aggrieved Excise Officer, in defending himself against the accusations made against his profession, commenced his retaliation with the words: 'Sir, – It would have been better if Mr Steel (whoever he may be) …', and went on to say that his department had nothing to do with adulteration on the publican's premises, and would have no such control until the 1st of January, 1873. Although the Excise was responsible for keeping the adulteration of spirits and other duty-bearing goods in check, its area of jurisdiction did not extend to the very place where the bulk of it was occurring.

Steel returned fire by demoting the Excise Officer to an Exciseman (on paper at any rate), and blamed the apparent misinterpretation of his initial letter on his drinking fusel-oil. Not to be outdone, the Excise Officer wrote back, still feeling aggrieved, probably more-so following the tittle-tattle that had erupted between the two combatants …

> … I have, unfortunately, been before his rubicund countenance on several occasions when he strung his high-flown and intensely dramatic phrases together, though little to my benefit. My remark, "whoever he may be," was simply a milder form of writing, "don't care who he may be." I would not have intruded again on your space, but at the urgent request of several brother officers, and beg to leave Mr Steel to tender mercies of abler heads and hands. – I am, etc.,

> NOT AN EXCISEMAN, BUT AN EXCISE OFFICER
> Port Dundas, Oct. 4.

Among the many letters that were published in the *'Mail* at the beginning of October, that from 'Guid Scots Drink' is worthy of a mention. It came during what may be termed the calm before the storm, and addressed the issue of fusel-oil, prune wine, and other relevant matters. In it, the writer challenged the notion that prune wine might be an adulterant, and said that on analysis by eminent chemists it had proved to be a perfectly pure and wholesome wine which was recommended as an article for greatly improving new whisky – 'because it volatilises the fusel oil above mentioned.' The same critic could not understand why French brandy should be used as an adulterant as the duty paid on it was slightly more than that paid on whisky, and this, combined with the additional costs of transporting it from France, would make it an unviable additive. This might be true of a pure and legitimate brandy from France, but as we have already seen brandy itself was subject to adulteration, and in back-street cellars any number of substances, including acetic ether, French wine vinegar, and perhaps even a dash of the real thing, might be stirred together to mimic this foreign spirit at a lesser cost. In the dilution of whisky with water, this cheap and spurious French brandy would have been one of many things added in an effort to bring some sort of taste and colour to an insipid nectar.

Professor Anderson Joins the Affray

Thomas Anderson did not wish to become involved with the arguments over whisky. He had other more pressing matters to attend to and, besides, why should he argue with a fellow scientist, one carrying out research at the same educational establishment, young – about eight years his junior – but nevertheless very experienced where chemical analysis was concerned. He had read the initial reports and each day's sprinkling of letters with some scepticism, and a great deal of interest, but the whole thing was verging on the ridiculous with councillors and officers of Her Majesty's Government trading insults in a national newspaper. It was time for a second learned party to intervene and logically deal with the various points that had given rise to the tempestuous arguments. Professor Anderson could hold himself back no longer.

Unfortunately, while attempting to install some rational thought into the controversy, Anderson only succeeded in adding to the complexity and confusion. His letter appeared in the *'Mail* on the 12th of October, and in it he indicated his liking for further details on how the analytical tests were carried out. The detection of methyl alcohol, he said, in the 'presence of ordinary ethylic alcohol is one of the most difficult problems of chemical analysis ....' He had certainly hit the nail on the head. He also reckoned that the amount of methyl alcohol in the naphtha used in making methylated spirits was only about 20 or 30 per cent, and that when ten parts of this naphtha was mixed with ninety of spirits of wine (or ethyl alcohol) to make methylated spirits, and then further 'diluted' in a spurious whisky mixture, the actual amount of methyl alcohol was so small as to defy any attempts at its detection.

The arguments start to get a bit technical from this stage onwards, and I have no wish to become bogged down in chemical formulae, percentages, and the like. However, this particular issue is of some importance, and I feel I must include certain details, even if solely to show how confusing the whole thing must have appeared to regular readers of the 'Mail.

It was, at that time, a purified form of naphtha that was used for methylation purposes, and while it wasn't 100 per cent pure and made entirely of methyl alcohol, it almost certainly had more than Anderson suggested. Someone hiding under the name of Nicol Jarvie later wrote to the 'Mail on two occasions to correct Anderson on this point, and indicated that the percentage of methyl alcohol in the naphtha used for methylation was of the order of at least 60 or 70, as analysed in the Excise laboratory. This still only means a difference of around 4 per cent, which might not seem a lot, but in the world of analytical science it was, and is, very substantial.

Anderson then demonstrated his lack of familiarity with the laws governing the sale of methylated spirits, the source of the methyl alcohol found in some samples. He said it could not be purchased by the man in the street, its use being restricted to those engaged in certain manufacturing activities who had permission from the Excise. He admitted that all the laws in the land would not stop its use by dishonest individuals, but while his interpretation of the statute-books might have been correct for the 1850s, he was far short of the mark for the year in question, and we will examine this in more detail in the next chapter.

It then seems that in his haste to put pen to paper, Anderson's skills in the art of reasoned and precise thought quite simply vanished. He continued ...

... the whole production of fousel oil in Scotland does not exceed

20,000 or 30,000 gallons a year, or less than one-third of a per cent of the spirit produced. Even if we suppose the whole of the fousel oil obtained in the Scotch distilleries to be accumulated in Glasgow, it would not amount to 2 per cent of the spirit consumed in the town. It would, however, be most erroneous to suppose that the whole fousel oil is consumed as an adulterant. A certain part of it goes to the manufacturers of fruit essences, and there are other perfectly legitimate uses to which it is applied, and I know it is a fact that in some of the largest distilleries in Scotland the entire production is so used. The statement, therefore, that a commission agent in Glasgow had sold 10,000 gallons in a single week, though possible, is highly improbable; but the inference to be drawn from the article in your columns, that sales on a similar scale are effected every week, is manifestly absurd.

All Anderson's words were in vain. Had he taken the time to read the 'Mail's report properly he would have saved himself an awful lot of time, and face – ' ... a single commission agent in this city in a single *month* disposed of 10,000 gallons of fousel oil ...'

This ability to make such blatant blunders appears to have been an inherent trait peculiar to analysts of the period; if they weren't arguing with each other, they were frequently fudging the facts. Dr James St. Clair Gray was criticised for one or two minor mistakes he made during the course of the whisky analysis, and it's nice to see that he was not alone in such behaviour.

On the subject of Berlin spirit and 'finish', Anderson pointed out that the former was a pure silent spirit which had not been imported for quite some time. It was 3d per gallon dearer than the best Scottish grain spirit and therefore unlikely to be used as an adulterant. Berlin spirit was not 'finish'. Again this was no doubt true, but who is to say that an impure version wasn't imported which avoided duty by being disguised as a varnish by the addition of shellac, the unsavoury mixture working out even cheaper, and more palatable to the unfortunate drinkers of the stuff, than methylated spirits-based varnish. Of course the thought of people drinking varnish sounds quite horrendous, but in fact some of these so-called varnishes, as we shall see later, had very little, and at times none, of the shellac gum. Of 'finish', Anderson said it was 'such a filthy compound that I should imagine it would not be tolerated except by the most thoroughly vitiated taste.' Here he was correct, although his underlying inference that it could never be used in whisky was quite wrong.

With all the questions that Professor Anderson has thrown up, especially in the area of methylated spirits and 'finish', and considering the number of whisky samples that contained either one or the other, it may now be wise to take a step backwards to look more closely at methylated spirits, what it is, when and why it originated, the controls governing its passage, and how it could possibly have found its way into shebeens and public houses in Glasgow.

4

The Origins of Methylated Spirits

IT is thought that methyl alcohol was first isolated by the chemist Robert Boyle in the mid-seventeenth century. The term 'methyl comes from the Greek words for wine and wood, and is an indication of the alcohol's original use and source.[1] A watery distillate known as pyroligneous acid, derived from the thermal decomposition of various hardwoods like maple or beech, was at one time refined or distilled to varying degrees to produce acetic acid, acetone, and methyl alcohol, the mixture being generally called either pyroxylic spirit, wood-spirit, methylic spirit, or wood-naphtha. The actual amount of methyl alcohol it contained varied greatly, and depended on the efficiency and extent of the purification process.

An embryonic version of what could almost be termed methylated spirits was brought to the attention of the Government in 1843 when it was discovered that duty-free consignments of naphtha, from abroad, often contained considerable proportions of drinkable spirit upon which duty would normally have been paid. In his paper titled *The Revenue in Jeopardy from Spurious Chemistry Demonstrated in Researches upon Wood-Spirit and Vinous-Spirit*, Doctor Andrew Ure gave a number of examples, one of which centred around eighteen casks of 'naphtha' from New York. While under scrutiny by Customs at Liverpool, doubts were raised as to the contents being genuine, and a sample was sent for analysis to Ure, who at that time was the Analytical Chemist to the Board of Customs. His results revealed that a rather small amount of pyroligneous acid had been mixed with a considerable volume of 'alcohol or strong whisky', so much so that one-hundred gallons of it would have contained 'the equivalent in spirits of 91 gallons proof strength.' This was clearly not naphtha. In the words of Ure – 'The spirits, thus distilled, may be rendered quite palatable by rectification with potash, so as to be fit for making English gin. The cargo of naptha,

78

of which said bottle is a sample, is, therefore, a fraudulent importation of spirits under the mask of pyroligneous acid.'

That might have been all very well had the story ended there, but, as was usual during this period, a lengthy debate ensued. First of all, the owners of the 'naphtha' had a sample analysed; Professor Graham of the London University, who carried out the tests, stating that it was not convertible into gin, was not alcohol, and contained no pyroligneous acid. A Liverpool chemist also found 'no evidence of the presence of alcoholic spirit', and said that it was solely wood-naphtha and could not be made into a drinkable liquid. Another chemist agreed.

Then the tide turned in favour of Doctor Ure. A Mr George Taylor was of the opinion that if redistilled, a spirit could be obtained which could be used for all the purposes that spirits of wine (alcohol) was then employed. One company examined a sample and declared that the liquid was indeed a spirit. A second firm backed this up by saying that it was 'common grain-spirit, mixed with tar.... The import of this article, if allowed at a less duty than paid on spirit by the English distiller, will have an injurious effect on the spirits of wine trade, and consequently also interfere with the revenue.'

Doctor Ure then analysed a completely different and unrelated batch of 'naphtha' and found it to contain ninety-five per cent alcohol.

> The admission of these pretended foreign naphthas, at the low duty hitherto charged, is most injurious to the spirits revenue, as also to the home manufacture of wood-spirit. Since alcohol is untaxed in France, Belgium, Germany, and America, it can be made in these countries of the above strength for less than two shillings a gallon, and when merely flavoured with wood or coal-naphtha, it is a far more valuable solvent of hatters' gums, than the genuine wood-spirit, which is so offensive to the workmen, that in many hat factories, alcohol would be preferred were its price only double that of wood-spirit. Indeed, the consumption of alcohol for dissolving hatters' gums and making varnishes, has been of late years entirely superseded by naphthalized spirits of wine, whether imported from foreign countries, or fraudulently compounded at home.

Although not called as such, spirits of wine, or alcohol, 'flavoured' with naphtha, was of course methylated spirits, but it was a few years before it was so labelled.

It must again be stressed that this was a very early period in the field of chemical analysis, and the above example, where analysts totally disagree with one another, aptly demonstrates the ambiguous nature of the chemistry that then existed. Almost twenty years later, Doctor James St. Clair Gray and Messrs Tatlock and Anderson would be arguing over similar matters in the detection of methyl alcohol.

Before 1855 the duty levied on spirits was so high that the financial incentive to obtain them from either illicit distillers, or in spurious importations like that uncovered by Ure, was considerable. In 1854 and 1855 whisky rose to double its former price and the man in the street was paying 6d per gill as opposed to the previous 3d[2]. Hat manufacturers and other trades who made much use of spirits were almost forced to utilise the wares of the back-street distiller. The Government was becoming increasingly concerned over the loss of revenue, and the matter was brought to a head in 1853 when the patentee of a lubricant applied for permission to receive duty-free spirit for use in his product.[3] In order to determine the practicability of supplying such spirits to various manufacturing industries, in March 1855 the Chairman of the Inland Revenue wrote to Professors Graham, Hofmann, and Redwood – three gentlemen who had some experience of mixed spirits – to request a full investigation into the chemistry and viability of the proposal. The main points for consideration were as follows:

1. It is absolutely necessary that means should be devised by which such spirit may first be rendered unfit for human consumption.
2. That spirit, after being thus treated, should still be so pure as to be generally available for the purposes to which it is to be applied in the arts and manufactures.
3. It should not be capable of purification by any simple process of rectification or otherwise, so as to be made palatable by the addition of sweetening or flavouring ingredients.
4. It is highly desirable, that while the mixed spirit should be rendered as offensive as possible to the taste or smell, no decidedly poisonous properties should be communicated.[4]

Professors Graham et al set to work. After extensive studies involving a number of chemical substances, it was discovered that the addition of wood-naphtha to spirits of wine met the desired criteria. Crude wood-naphtha was first tried, but it was thought that a purer version would be more suited to trade use due to the reduced quantity of oils and other components which might conceivably interfere with the quality of the resin with which it was mixed.

This comparatively pure wood-naphtha was supplied by Messrs Turnbull & Co of Glasgow, and was normally sold at 8s 6d per gallon. When five per cent of it was added to strong alcohol, its presence was easily detected by its taste and odour, and it was thought that this was more than sufficient to render spirits unsaleable as a beverage. Varnishes made with it dried readily and had no residual smell or peculiar characteristics. In addition, there was no known means of separating the methyl alcohol so as to make the remaining spirits of wine drinkable.

Unfortunately, Graham et al seem to have ignored the fourth requirement, and 'poisonous properties' *were* communicated to the spirit through the addition of methyl alcohol, although perhaps its effects were not fully understood at the time. As the *North British Daily Mail* said in its second part of the 1872 whisky report, methyl alcohol gives rise to very different reactions within the human frame from the more common and drinkable ethyl alcohol, the symptoms being described as 'maniacal'. As well as the typical manifestations of poisoning by any alcohol or narcotic poison, the drinker's nervous and muscular systems become partially paralysed. He develops an 'intense feeling of languor,' and 'the muscles seem to lose their tone and elasticity, giving rise to the loose, slouching, irregular, and tottering gait with which persons resident in Glasgow are unhappily too well conversant.' While spirits of wine with five per cent of this purified wood-naphtha was found to fit the bill, it was felt that ten per cent would be preferable so as to prevent the identifiable smell from being disguised by other odorous substances. This alcoholic mixture was christened 'methylated spirit'.

Further tests were conducted to determine just how unpalatable this new discovery would be when mixed with public house spirits. The Government was aware of the very real possibility of such misuse and wished to protect its revenue. Mr G. Smith, a London distiller who was approached for advice, was of the opinion that 'publicans would never use such a spirit for mixing with their liquors, even in a small proportion.' In his own tests, Smith came to the conclusion that a mixture of gin with one-eighth part of the methylated spirits was nauseous and unpalatable. Even with one-sixteenth part, the flavour was 'still very strongly marked', and was indeed still perceptible at a dilution of 1 in 64. With such small dilution it was felt that the monetary saving made by the publican would be no compensation for the deterioration in the quality of his gin. Whisky was a different matter entirely, and a cautious note was added to warn of possible abuse; its 'smoky flavour' might very easily disguise the tang of meths.

It was recommended that the new spirit should be made by distillers and rectifiers who were sanctioned by the Inland Revenue, and all other persons wishing to commence manufacture could only do so by taking out an Excise licence. The Excise would have complete control (or so they thought) of every aspect of its use, including the monitoring of naphtha quality so as to ensure uniformity within every batch. On the retail side, oil-men and druggists would be supplied either directly from the distiller or through the agency of a wholesale druggist or drysalter. Everything seemed to be taken care of and the Government, after one or two questions to the investigating scientists, was ready to go.

On the 26th June 1855 an Act of Parliament was passed, and 'methylated spirit' was thrust into Victorian life. Most of the points raised in the previous scientific report were catered for. The cost of a licence for making the new spirit was £10 10s, and no less than 500 gallons were to be made at any one time in a building or warehouse approved by the Inland Revenue. Its comings and goings were to be strictly monitored and records kept – all deliveries and receipts were to be accompanied by the appropriate paperwork, and the spirit was to be transported in containers holding no more than ten gallons. Every person receiving it from the makers was to produce a certificate signed by an Excise Officer to verify that he was licensed to receive it. Paperwork followed the spirit everywhere. As was usual with such legislation, the wording in the clauses was extremely complex and designed to cover every conceivable loophole.

The Act came into force in October of that year. By the 31st March 1856 a total of 76,049 proof gallons had been made, 27,398 of them in Scotland. There were ten licensed methylators in England and none in Scotland and Ireland, the spirit being made in these countries by certain distillers and rectifiers.[5] Many illicit distillers went out of business due to the fact that manufacturing trades who used spirits could now obtain them just as cheap legally.

The duty on drinkable spirits was increasing all the time. Between 1852 and 1857 there was a rise of 118 per cent, and yet the volume of home-made spirits consumed in Scotland was practically identical for the two years, standing at around seven million gallons. The increase in revenue from spirits for the same period was of the order of one million pounds.[6] Whisky was such a popular drink in Scotland that the true Scot was obviously not turned from his favourite tipple by a mere difference in price. While this was true, and there were those whose financial circumstances could accommodate the extra, the lower classes were finding themselves increasingly isolated and unable to afford the real McCoy. With the reduction in the number of illicit distillers, where could the poorer working man and his unscrupulous publican turn? The answer was, of course, to the retailers of methylated spirits.

Indian Whiskee

In 1861 the Government saw fit to remove some of the restrictions imposed on the sale of methylated spirits, and an amending Act was passed. Now any person, barring those who were distillers, rectifiers, or retailers of beer, wine, or spirits, could, on payment of £2 2s, obtain a licence to sell up to one gallon to anyone. It was a case of lighting the blue touch-paper and standing well back. To nip any potential explosion of abuse in the bud, a separate clause was added which basically said that if anyone coloured, purified, flavoured, mixed or prepared methylated spirits in any way that might allow its use as a beverage, they would be find £100.

Druggists were the main retailers of methylated spirits and it was to them that the public turned when, for whatever reason, a supply was required. It was used in a variety of ways including being burnt in lamps as a source of heat, or, when mixed with oil of turpentine, as a source of light.[7] (Oil of turpentine burns with a very smoky, but none-the-less luminous, flame, and from the 1830s it had been mixed with alcohol so as to reduce this smokiness and give brightness to the non-luminous flame of the latter.) All too frequently it found its way into medicines destined for use internally, even although this was not recommended by Graham et al in the 1855 report; the practice was later banned in 1866. Mixed with shellac or some other gum, it formed a thin varnish called 'finish' which was much used by hat makers and furniture polishers alike.

It might appear peculiar to us today to learn of druggists selling varnish, but at that time they dealt in all manner of goods from medicines and poisons to curry powders and mosquito cures. They sold everything, much of it made on the premises to their own individual recipe.

While a licence was needed to sell methylated spirits on its own, once mixed with something else – like oil of turpentine or shellac – there was no control over its sale and a licence was not required. A money-pinching druggist of low morals might save himself £2 2s by retailing 'finish' in which the amount of gum contained therein was minimal, and at times totally lacking. In other words he would be selling methylated spirits under a false label, something which he could be, and often was, fined, even although he had purchased the so-called 'finish' from a wholesale dealer in good faith. This did take place, but some simply used it as an excuse, and it was only those who were able to produce receipts and invoices, stating that it *was* reputedly 'finish', that were dealt with sympathetically by the courts. A test was available to the druggist to allow him to easily determine whether there was enough gum in his 'finish', so there really was no excuse, even in mitigating circumstances. In the same way, he might add a mere hint of oil of turpentine, call the mixture 'burning fluid', or whatever, and sell unlimited quantities to whoever should desire it.

The owner of a public house or shebeen who was finding the increased price of whisky too much to bear, could then obtain duty-free spirit at a fraction of the cost of the genuine duty-paying article. What did it matter if it contained a little turpentine or shellac gum? By the time he had added some fusel-oil and various other ingredients including, perhaps, even a tot of real whisky, his customers would not notice the difference. As far as he was concerned, the fact that patients in hospitals received methylated spirits as the spirit-base for their internal medicines meant that he need have no fear of shoving it down the throats of the public. It was all part and parcel of his perfectly safe, and cheap, 'House Blend'.

Of course the man in the street did not necessarily have to visit his local howff to buy a few glasses of oblivion. His friendly druggist could supply, as has already been said, almost all his needs, and there are cases recorded where methylated spirits was sold for drinking, either flavoured with peppermint or as part of grand-sounding concoctions like 'Concentrated Essence of Indian Brandee'.[8]

It was difficult for the Inland Revenue to obtain convictions in this area. Many druggists were unsure of exactly what the law was saying, and sundry letters were sent to Somerset House, the Inland Revenue's laboratory, for clarification. While legitimate confusion did exist, there were some who sought to thumb their nose at authority by hiding behind a feigned mask of ignorance.

Battles were being fought in the courts with increasing regularity. A typical example took place in Bristol in 1866 when, on the 8th of January, an Excise Officer entered the shop of a Mr Sharland and asked if he sold methylated spirits. The reply was "Yes," and he then ordered a half-pint flavoured with oil of peppermint, for which he paid 9d. With great skill the lawyer for the defence manipulated the words of the law to show that his client had committed no offence. Although the selling of flavoured methylated spirits for drinking was not allowed, the officer who had made the purchase had not mentioned that it was to used as such. In addition, the liquid was no longer solely methylated spirits, and a licence was therefore not needed for its sale. His argument was illustrated in the example of a cook who mixed brandy with his mince-pies, but was not required to take out a spirits licence. A mitigated penalty of £12 10s was incurred, although the Bench recommended that the Inland Revenue remit the whole.[9]

In another case a similar mixture, labelled 'Finish half-pint, oil of peppermint half-drachm', was found to contain methylated spirits and peppermint, but none of the gum which should have been present had true 'finish' been used. We will look more closely at this problem towards the end of this chapter.

The main point here is that many internal medicines were made up with methylated spirits – a usage which was sanctioned by the Inland Revenue, as exemplified in a letter to one Alfred Bird of Birmingham in 1863. In it, the Board stated that they 'did not object to the manufacture and sale of any strictly pharmaceutical preparation, made with methylated spirits, so long as such preparations were used for medical purposes only, and not so made and sold as a cover for use as a beverage.'[10]

In the eyes of the law it was exceedingly difficult to differentiate between a beverage and drinkable medicine, as it could be argued that every beverage had some sort of beneficial effect – even whisky had certain health-giving properties attached to it. As a result, many druggists sold their fancy-sounding medicinal potions knowing full well that they were to be consumed for their spirituous content and not used to cure some ailment.

Chemists, or druggists, were, on the whole, opposed to the use of methylated spirits in internal medicines. Instances occasionally took place in which the full extent of its use was brought to light, and great horror was displayed by one and all, perhaps rather falsely in some cases. During one particular trial the magistrate expressed his astonishment when it was disclosed that in 1864 the South Staffordshire Hospital had put out a contract to tender in which it was stipulated that thirty-six of the listed tinctures were to be made with methylated spirits. It then emerged that it was used extensively 'by the great body of surgeons and dispensers in the United Kingdom.'[11] Hospitals adopting such practices were accused of caring more about cheap spirits than the health of their patients. The whole thing was said to be disgraceful and an example of gross adulteration – 'no respectable chemist would use it.'

Another important case raised its head in 1866 when it became known to the Inland Revenue that a number of chemists in the north of England were selling methylated spirits without a licence. Charles McRae, the Supervisor of the Excise in Wolverhampton, was despatched to the chemist and druggist shop of Mr Thomas Reade where he asked for something called 'Indian Essence'. Mr Reade's preparation was of some renown in the area and was attractively packaged and presented in bottles bearing labels which extolled its virtues.

> Reade's Original Indian Essence, a pleasant and effectual medicine, warming and comforting – Antispasmodic, Astringent, Diaphoretic, and Diuretic. Perfectly free from any injurious drugs, and may, therefore, be taken with the greatest confidence. Dose: Adults, one tablespoonful, to be repeated when required; children, one or two teaspoonfuls. Prepared by Thomas Reade, chemist, 9 Cock Street, Wolverhampton. Only threepence per ounce.[12]

On analysis at Somerset House the liquid was found to contain methylated spirits and a little chloroform sweetened with either treacle or course brown sugar. The lawyer for the defence stated that his client was a respectable chemist who 'had had the good fortune, for the benefit of suffering humanity, to invent a medicine called Reade's Indian Essence… ' This was dearer than brandy or gin, and so was meant as medicine and not a cheap and drinkable spirit alternative.

Accordingly, Mr Reade thought himself within the law, but the Inland Revenue was having none of it. Their spokesman said that methylated spirits could only be used with those medicinal preparations recognised by the *British Pharmacopoeia*. Concoctions like 'Indian Brandee' and 'Indian Whiskee' were not listed and were 'prepared and sold for dram-drinking purposes all over the country.' This was later backed up in an article which said that the practice of using methylated spirits in medicines soon descended to the manufacture of compounds with names which were 'more suggestive of the gin palace than of the druggist's shop' – 'Indian Brandee, Indian Tincture, Gindee, Whiskee, and the like.'[13]

There then followed the now familiar series of arguments with one professor saying that the Essence had been made up from nitrous ether, or sweet spirits of nitre, chloroform, treacle, golden syrup, essence of ginger, capsicum, and infusion of gentian. An essential element of nitrous ether was methylated spirits, so the latter was therefore added, not directly, but as part of the ether. The Inland Revenue had perhaps looked for methyl alcohol, found it, and jumped to the wrong conclusion as to how it got there. The whole thing was very complicated. At the end of what was an important dispute in highlighting the use of methylated spirits in medicines, the case was dismissed, although not without a few cardinal words of wisdom from the magistrate.

> Three chemists had been called, and had differed in their evidence, as chemists always did, when employed on opposite sides. It was, he regretted to say, found to be the case that scientific men could always take a scientific view according to the wishes of the party whose cause they were engaged to support; and science was not yet so certain but that they might do so conscientiously.

Further legislation was passed in 1866, to come into effect in January 1867, but instead of clearing up a lot of the existing confusion it only made things worse. There were two relevant clauses with which to put matters right. The first dealt directly with medicines intended for internal use and made it an offence for anyone to employ 'methylated spirit or any derivative thereof' in such preparations. Even before the new Act was operational a serious flaw was revealed in that the distinction between medicines for internal and external use was said to be doubtful. A number of methylated linaments that were intended for external application could be used internally, and for this reason a wide door would be thrown open to fraudulent practices.

There was much discussion among pharmacists regarding what was seen as a breakdown in the Inland Revenue's control over the use of methylated spirits. At one particular meeting a resolution was adopted, and a copy sent to the Board of Inland Revenue, in which the industry's fears were expressed and urgent demands made for some new system to more securely prevent 'the conversion of a duty-free spirit into an imitation of pure spirit, on which duty is paid.'[14]

The second clause of the Act tackled 'finish'.

> If any Person shall, after any Methylated Spirit shall have been mixed with Gum Resin for forming the Mixture known as 'Finish,' or any like Mixture, separate the Gum Resin from the said Methylated Spirit, or alter the said Mixture in any Manner except by adding thereto a further Quantity of Gum Resin, or any Article for the sole Purpose of colouring the same, he shall forfeit the Sum of Two hundred Pounds, and the said Spirit and Mixture respectively so separated or altered as aforesaid shall be forfeited, together with the Vessels or other Packages containing the same.[15]

A Lack of Shellac

It wasn't long before letters from chemists hit the pages of their trade periodical, *The Pharmaceutical Journal*. Some displayed concern and a desire to learn the facts surrounding the new Act, while others revealed a knowledge which they wished to share with their brethren. Copies of correspondence with the Inland Revenue formed a part of many of these, and there existed a united front in evading the clutches of a wavering law which might just as easily taint the innocent as the guilty.

One letter, dated September 1866, echoed the confusion that had arisen regarding methylated spirits and 'methylated finish' (or simply 'finish'). The writer reminded his colleagues that to sell the former they needed a licence, but for the latter they did not, and the new legislation had no affect on this whatsoever. He advised all chemists to test their 'finish' to ensure that it had the mandatory minimum of one ounce of shellac or sandarac for every gallon of spirits. Any less, and it could no longer be termed 'finish'. [16]

It was generally accepted among druggists that the retailing of 'finish' was one way in which they could sell methylated spirits without a licence, and it was therefore in their interest to have as little of the shellac in it as the Excise would allow. Initially the Board of Inland Revenue had issued an order to the effect that 'the solution must contain not less than three ounces of shellac or other resinous substance in every gallon to entitle it to the name of 'finish'.[17] However, the Board was then informed that 'when made of this strength it was unsuited to some of the purposes for which it was required, and accordingly the strength was reduced to one ounce to the gallon.'

In 1867 druggists were actively encouraged to take out a methylated spirits licence through the combined reduction of the fee to 10s and the Inland Revenue's change to the original three ounces of shellac in a gallon of 'finish'. The larger proportion of gum would have made it easier to detect – whether by the druggist or the authorities – and it was felt that many would simply pay the cost and avoid the risk of prosecution. Although a lesser fee, the Government may have found an increase in revenue in this area as a result of the large number of druggists who had previously sold just 'finish' and were now licensed for methylated spirits.

This alteration in the composition of 'finish' was followed by numerous spot-checks by Excise Officers. The Pharmaceutical Society had apparently not had sufficient warning of the new order so as to inform its members, and consequently many were caught out. Of thirteen samples obtained from different localities, only one contained the proper quantity of resin.[18] The blame was laid squarely at the door of manufacturers and, once again, all chemists were reminded to carry out tests on all delivered batches so as to keep themselves right. It was the druggist who would be fined – not the manufacturer.

The practice of selling 'finish', with a minimal amount of shellac gum, as an alternative to methylated spirits became so prevalent that some people came to believe that shellac was an essential ingredient of the latter. Methylated spirits and 'finish' became, in some quarters, synonymous, and many myths and inaccuracies grew up around them.

In a court case highlighted in *The Chemist and Druggist* on the 15th July 1876, Mr Micks, who was 'collector of Inland Revenue at Hull', gave some historical background in which he said that the composition of methylated spirits was spirits of wine, naphtha, and *gum*. Now this is clearly very strange, and quite wrong. In 1879 another case was reported in the same periodical in which a solicitor, in defending a druggist charged with selling methylated spirits without a licence, said that the gum was added to make the spirit more nauseous and further prevent people from drinking it. This, again, is very peculiar, as the purpose of the gum was to transform the spirit into a thin varnish. That said, the three ounces per gallon was excessive, where certain legitimate users were concerned, so why it was later increased from one ounce back to the original three is a bit of a mystery, unless there is a certain amount of truth in the above story. Was the abuse of methylated spirits so much of a problem that a reduction in the quality of varnishes used by hatters and furniture polishers was the only answer? Apparently so, although the quality would not presumably have been affected too much, and besides, if some of these trades had obtained their spirit from illicit distillers before 1855, you can be sure they would have no qualms about ordering and receiving their 'finish' in which the amount of shellac was exactly as *they* had stipulated, and not the authorities. The Board of Inland Revenue was not making hats!

And so that was the situation regarding methylated spirits, as it stood, in 1872. It should now be quite plain that much of what Professor Anderson said in his letter to the *North British Daily Mail*, especially with regard to 'finish' and the retail of its gumless cousin, fell far short of the truth. There can be no doubt that he was an intelligent and well-educated man of some distinction, but in this case it seems that he set foot in something which he knew nothing about, his words only serving to set him up for criticism from other followers of the whisky disclosure. Perhaps he acted like many persons who have the good fortune to occupy an elevated and privileged social position in that they *think* they know all the details regarding a particular subject, but in fact know very little of how that subject *really* affects, or is dealt with by, the man in the street.

In exposing the scandalous condition of Glasgow's public house whisky, the '*Mail's* report also drew attention to the abuse of methylated spirits, but sadly the problem did not then go away. Even today there is a small number of people who drink the poison, the only differing and questionable ray of optimism being that these poor, unfortunate souls do so knowingly and it is not hidden behind the good name of Scotland's national drink.

5

Druggists – In at the 'Finish'

AS the main retailers of methylated spirits and sundry drugs and chemicals used in the adulteration of food and drink in the mid-Victorian period, druggists had a lot to answer for. It could be argued that their role was merely that of a merchant and that the law did not require them to know how such-and-such a product was to be used once it left the shop, but many were fully aware of what was going on, their only concern being to line their pockets as swiftly and effortlessly as possible.

In addition to the above and the more mundane consumables needed for everyday living, like lamp burning-fluid, ointments and pastes for maintaining horse-tackle, extracts for the hair, polish, pills and potions for curing every ailment known to man, and a million-and-one other compounds, they also supplied opium (in the form of a tincture termed laudanum), ether, and other intoxicating drugs and chemicals with which people would attempt to temporarily extricate themselves from the drudgeries of life. Poisons like strychnine, arsenic, and belladonna formed a part of many mixtures, and often mistakes were made which resulted in the death of the recipient. This can be aptly illustrated by the incident which took place in Somerset in the late 1860s in which two hundred sheep died after being dipped in a liquid that contained excessive amounts of the usually present arsenic.[1]

To give an idea of the range of items sold, it may be interesting to take a close look at a Glasgow druggist's recipe book dating to around the early 1870s. The druggist in question is C.B. Flint, who occupied premises at 209 and 211 Victoria Street (now Byres Road). According to the Glasgow Post Office Directory, Flint traded here from 1877/78, but the older recipes are almost certainly pre-1874 and may be either his notes when trading from an earlier location, or perhaps passed down to him from his father. I have added details in brackets to explain certain terms.

FOOT ROT IN SHEEP

Verdigris – (a basic acetate of copper, commonly seen as the greenish 'rust' on copper or brass)
Alum – (a mineral salt)
Blue Vitriol – (copper sulphate)
Corrosive Sub – (highly poisonous mercuric chloride)
Copperas – (iron sulphate)
Vinegar

OINTMENT OR PASTE FOR HARNESS

Yellow wax – 8oz
Indigo Blue – (a dye) – 1oz
Ivory Black – (a black powder, originally made from burnt ivory, and also from bone.) – 2oz
Soft Soap – (soap containing potash) – 8oz
Turpentine – 4oz

CURE FOR MOSQUITOES

Pine or Juniper sawings
Artemisia leaves powdered – (a genus of bitter-tasting plants including wormwood)
Tobacco and a small quantity of Arsenic

VEGETABLE EXTRACT FOR THE HAIR

Oleum Ricini – (castor-oil) – 8oz
Eau de Cologne – 12oz
Ess. Bergamotte – (a type of citron or orange whose aromatic rind yields an oil used in perfumery) – 1oz
(illegible ingredient) – 8oz
Alcohol 60.o.p. ad Winch.26 – 80oz

ORIENTAL PERFUME

Sp. of Wine – (alcohol)
Ess. Ambergris – (a strongly scented substance found floating on the sea and in the intestines of the spermaceti whale)
Bergamotte
Oleum Lavand – (oil of lavender)
Oleum Sandalwood – (a fragrant oil from a tropical wood)
Oleum Lemon

Ess. (Moschi?) – (probably the essence of a small musk-like plant)
Ess. (Messam?) – (indistinct and illegible ingredient)
(?) Roses
Mellis – (may be a honey or sweet smelling essence)

FURNITURE OIL

Oleum Lini – (probably linseed oil)
Sweet Ale
White of Eggs (2) and mix well

VARNISH

Sp. of Wine
Shellac – a dark red transparent resin produced on the twigs of trees in the East by insects, which is then melted, strained, and formed into thin plates.)
Gum Juniper
Gum Mastic – (a pale yellow resin from the lentisk tree)

WHITE SPIRIT VARNISH

Mastic – 18oz
Junipers
Methylated Alcohol – 2 Galls

GINGER WINE

Alcohol – $2^1/2$ Galls	Rum – $1^1/2$ Galls
Sugar	Orange Peel
Lemon Juice	Water – 6 Galls

Isinglass – (a glutinous substance, chiefly prepared from the air-bladders of the sturgeon)

Ginger Root	Lemon Peel

Other notable recipes include firework-type concoctions like 'Green Fire', 'Red Fire', and 'Fire Balls'; toothache cures containing shellac, camphor and chloroform; a 'Stimulating Embrocation' whose ingredients include acetic acid, turpentine, and the yolk of an egg; an 'Influenza Mixture' containing morphine and belladonna; 'Mr Crispin's Currie Powder'; and hair-washes individually tailored for customers like Rosemary Caulharidis, Mrs Wingate, and Dr Rainy.[2] Hand-written in pencil, this chemist's recipe book is a pure delight to read through and is somehow evocative of an era that died out with Queen Victoria. Incidentally, the last hair-wash is rather curious as Dr James St. Clair

Gray was Harry Rainy's Assistant for a few years, the professor's long and flowing locks featuring prominently in photographs of the period. There were, of course, other 'Rainy' surnames in Glasgow, but a gut-feeling tells me that this preparation was for Harry.

It is also interesting to see a chemist selling alcoholic Ginger Wine and varnishes containing methylated spirits. One has to presume that Flint did not sell, or have a licence to sell, the latter, as the law stated that it was not permissible where alcoholic beverages were also sold. Nevertheless, he had it in stock for use in various recipes and you can see just how tempting it might be to substitute a gallon of the cheaper methylated spirits for the regular alcohol.

Many quack medicines, or cure-alls, were nothing more than coloured water, sometimes with added flavouring, and occasionally laced with narcotics like alcohol or opium. They certainly didn't cure half of the ailments that they were supposed to, but the patient would feel his or her malady slowly subsiding as they drifted into a subliminal state of drug-induced euphoria. Sometimes addiction would follow such a course of 'treatment', and in this way the addition of intoxicants was one way of ensuring a steady trickle of customers at the druggist's door. 'Godfrey's Elixer,' one of many popular Victorian remedies, contained a pint of laudanum in every three gallons.[3] In 1867, during a lecture delivered by a Dr Hawkins at King's Lynn, it was revealed that a chemist in that town regularly sold five to six gallons of this elixer every week. Other chemists were selling similar volumes of laudanum each week and as much as 200 lbs of solid opium in a year. A druggist might have a drawer full of opium in half drachm packets ready for sale, and it was not unusual for customers to consume three in a day; indeed one woman, also staying in King's Lynn, was known to take a quarter of an ounce of Turkey opium every day, a habit she had nurtured for several years. Many people would call in for an ounce-and-a-half of laudanum, drink it at the counter, and call back later in the day for a top-up.

In an early nineteenth century magazine article titled *De Quincey's amazing Confessions of an English Opium Eater*, the author said that no one could ever return to drinking alcohol after 'experiencing the wondrous sensations derived from so refined a stimulant as opium.' There were in fact several reasons for the alarming increase in opium consumption in the mid-Victorian period, none of which are linked to the above.

℞ Pulv. Opii Rect
(Swan & Proctor)

RECTIFIED OPIUM

Is Turkey Opium of Standard Quality.

It is distinguished from crude Opium of commerce by its freedom from Narcotine, Fat, Caoutchouc, and odorous matter, *and by its unvarying strength as regards Morphia,* of which alkaloid it invariably contains 10 per cent. when powdered, or 9 per cent. when in mass.

The Trade will find the above Powder the most satisfactory kind of Opium for preparing the tincture, sedative solution, and, indeed, for every pharmaceutical preparation into which Opium enters.

Present Price—Powder, 30s. per lb.; Mass, in 1-lb. Blocks, 27s., subject to fluctuation.

To be had through all Wholesale Firms, or from the Patentees,

SWAN & PROCTOR,

MANUFACTURING PHARMACISTS,

NEWCASTLE-ON-TYNE.

Opium was widely used in many medicinal preparations in the nineteenth century, and was seen by some as a cheaper stimulant alternative to alcohol. (*Mitchell Library*).

Opium was initially used by the upper and middle classes, but the increasing price of alcohol was one factor which gradually attracted those in the lower echelons of society who saw it as a cheaper alternative to their public house tipple – and here we can see certain parallels with whisky and its adulteration. Another reason is that the Government was clamping down on the opening hours of public houses, and when his howff was shut, the man in the street could simply turn to his local druggist for a bottle of 'finish', a glass of laudanum, or a packet of opium.

The Forbes Mackenzie Act, passed in 1853, was the main culprit responsible for limiting licensing hours. Publicans were compelled to close their premises on Sundays and at a much earlier hour – 11 p.m. – during the week, a measure designed to reduce the amount of drunkenness on the streets and to make it safer and more pleasant for upright citizens to take their daily stroll. While the Act did have a beneficial effect, and the number of drunks was greatly reduced, there was a corresponding increase in the number of illicit liquor shops, and both they and the druggists found themselves doing a roaring trade supplying alcohol and drugs for a very real demand.

The 1853 Act was severely criticised for driving much of the late-night and Sunday drinking underground, and for forcing certain members of the lower classes to drink liquor that was more likely to be poisonous in such uncontrolled surroundings. Whether at the shebeen or the druggist's door, today's term, 'What's your poison?', was literally accurate. James Stirling's *Failure of the Forbes Mackenzie Act*, published in 1859, took a close look at the Act's many pitfalls and examined man's ability to get exactly what he wanted, whatever the law.

> But illicit selling is not the sole mode of evading a spirit law. There are other means of evasion, which, if less illegal, are perhaps more injurious. If we shut out those who will have drink from public-houses we only drive them into private houses...
>
> If spirits are forbidden, drugs may be used. Alcohol is not the only stimulant by which the craving of the drunkard may be stilled: opium, in the shape of laudanum, is cheaper, more powerful, and, though not under the ban of the law, infinitely more hurtful. That this mode of evading the Public-house Act prevails, to a greater or less extent, there cannot be a doubt, though statistical proof is wanting. The increase of laudanum-drinking in our large cities is a well-ascertained fact; and certainly nothing can more directly tend to stimulate this, the worst form of dissipation, than the unwise obstacles thrown in the way of spirit-drinking by a narrow-minded legislation.[4]

There were no restrictions on the sale of opium before 1868, and even after that date – when the Pharmacy Act was passed – they were limited to instructions in connection with labelling. Bottle labels had to bear the word 'Poison' and other basic information like the title of the contents and the name and address of the seller. Opium, and its preparations, was listed in Part II of the Act, Part I containing the more toxic substances like arsenic, cyanide, and strychnine. If the opium formed part of a medicine, as opposed to being sold on its own, then

William Dale's Botanic Medical Hall at 40 Queen Street, Glasgow, in 1906. This druggist's shop would have looked much the same in the mid-Victorian period when it was known to exist at the same address, and is largely representative of the form such premises took at that time. (*Graham Collection, Mitchell Library*).

none of the Act's recommendations applied, the only advice being that a prescription-book should be kept to contain the name of the person to whom the medicine was sold, and that the retailer's name and address should be included on the bottle label.

The Pharmacy Act was passed at a time when death by poisoning was a fairly regular occurrence. A person could walk into a druggist's shop and buy a bottle of arsenic or strychnine just as easily as he might buy a bottle of ginger beer, and such poisons often featured in murder cases. Children were also at risk. It was the simplest and most effective way of lulling a howling child to give it some laudanum-laced preparation; carelessness in administering often leading to grave consequences.

Patent medicines, the contents of which were kept a closely guarded secret both to prevent copying and to maintain the mystery which surrounded their watery ingredients, were still sold after 1868. A typical example was Doctor J. Collis Browne's 'Chlorodyn', an effective Victorian pain-killing mixture comprising chloroform, hydrochlorate of morphia (morphia, or morphine, being the chief narcotic derived from opium), extract of belladonna, hydrocyanic (or prussic) acid, capsicine (a peppery substance found in Capsicum), sulphuric ether, essence of peppermint, tobacco or Indian hemp (the latter being Cannabis or hashish), water or spirit and water, and treacle.[5] Some of these were designed specifically for children, and as the word 'Poison' was not included on their label, mothers assumed them to be relatively safe. As can be seen, this was not the case. There were many child deaths linked to such mixtures.

The low-level illumination produced by gas-lighting was another factor that led to the accidental swallowing of poisons, and this was one area in which the 1868 Act fell down. It was no use having the word 'Poison' on the label if it was often difficult to read due to a lack of light. In addition, many working-class people could not read, and so yet again we see legislation that failed a certain section of the population.

> An inquest has been held by Mr. Bedford, in St. James's Workhouse, on Henry C.T. Webb, of Little Windmill Street, who died from the effects of a large dose of laudanum, given by mistake for cough mixture. The laudanum had been used by the father of the deceased for poultices to relieve rheumatism, and the servant had placed that bottle beside the

FREEMAN'S CHLORODYNE

THE ORIGINAL AND ONLY TRUE.

Discovered and Invented by RICHARD FREEMAN in 1844.

It is one of those preparations so well known as having something in its composition which defies the imitator, and makes it an invaluable remedy. No other remedy known can be exhibited with so much confidence as a SEDATIVE, an ANTI-SPASMODIC, an ASTRINGENT, an ANODYNE, or DIAPHORETIC.

In its composition and effect it bears no resemblance to any of the many formulæ published, but has curative and chemical properties peculiarly its own, nor is there any analytical test for it. It has been found by the Profession and large numbers of the public to succeed after all imitations had failed, and maintains its unaltered position as the only reliable CHLORODYNE.

The following are presented as specimens of the many communications received by R. F. :—

From JOHN TANNER, M.D L.R.C.P., M.R.C.S., L.S.A., L.M., Physician to the Farringdon Dispensary.

"It gives me great pleasure to bear testimony in favour of FREEMAN'S Chlorodyne. I have prescribed it extensively, and find it in every respect far superior to any of the spurious compounds sold under the name of Chlorodyne. In cases of Asthma, Chronic Bronchitis, the last stage of Phthisis, and the Winter Cough of the Aged, I have never found any substitute or chemical combination its equal; moreover, in all cases where a sedative is required, it is a certain, safe, and agreeable remedy."

From DAVID EASTON, M.D., B.A., L.R.C.S., Medical Officer to the Rhins of Galloway Poorhouse, Stranraer, Wigtonshire, Scotland.

"I consider your Chlorodyne a valuable remedy. It has succeeded perfectly in those cases in which I have used it. In its action it is uniform, and in its effects most efficacious."

From C. SWABY SMITH, M.R.C.S. Eng., L.S.A., Surgeon to the Berks and Hants Extension Railway Works and Pewsey Union Author of "On the Treatment of Diphtheritic Sore Throat," &c.

"Having been in the habit of using Mr. FREEMAN's Chlorodyne for some time past, I have much pleasure in stating that *it has never failed to have the desired effect* in whatever case it has been administered."

IMPORTANT CAUTION.—Four Chancery Suits terminated in favour of FREEMAN'S ORIGINAL CHLORODYNE and against Collis Browne and Davenport. Lord Chancellor Selbourne, Lord Justice James, and Lord Justice Mellish condemned their proceedings, and decreed them to pay all costs. Reports of the suits in "Times," January 12 and July 13, 1864, and April 29 and July 24, 1873, and "British Medical Journal," May 3, 1873.

Sold in Bottles, 1s. 1½d.; 2 oz., 2s. 9d.; 4 oz., 4s. 6d.; 8 oz., 9s.; 10 oz., 11s.; and 20 oz., 20s. each; and for dispensing only in bottles, fl. 8 oz. 8s., and fl. 20 oz. 18s. (in weight one pound and a half). A liberal discount allowed. Special quotations given for quantities for Hospitals, Workhouses, Infirmaries, and other Public Medical Institutions. Full directions in various languages.

SOLE MANUFACTURER—

RICHARD FREEMAN, PHARMACIST, 70 KENNINGTON PARK ROAD, LONDON, S.E.

This advertisement for 'Chlorodyne' is one of many, each maker purporting to produce the original version of a pain-killing mixture whose ingredients included hashish, morphine,sulphuric ether, chloroform, and many others. (*Mitchell Library*).

cough mixture, where the mother had put it in case of need during the night. The child coughed excessively, and the mother, taking the bottle supposed to contain the mixture, administered a teaspoonful of laudanum. Medical aid was called in immediately the mistake was discovered, but without success. Verdict, "Accidental Death."[6]

It was a few years before distinctive 'Poison' bottles emerged bearing embossed decoration which made their identification much easier by touch alone.

All this talk about druggists might seem quite unrelated to whisky, but it helps to illustrate a small segment of the Victorian world, and allows us to view Glasgow's spirituous problem in its proper context, as one of many difficulties faced by a society who at that time were only beginning to implement, and come to grips with, proper legislation aimed at controlling its food, drink, and drugs. Many of the laws failed miserably, but they were a necessary starting-point upon which more effective legislation was later based.

Besides, at times whisky and the druggist were inextricably bound, 'Cholera Mixtures' and other popular Sunday potions occasionally containing some of the real McCoy, unlike 'Whiskee' and other drinks which probably contained none. Speaking in 1887, *The Scottish Wine, Spirit and Beer Trades' Review* remarked on the incidence of illicit spirit selling and the activities of druggists, and said that the law was winning the battle against many undesirable practices – unlike the 1870s...

> The chemist no longer secretly vends 'a poisoned poison behind his crimson lights,' or, in every-day phrase, his medical glass does not disguise whisky under the name of a tonic, as at one time was a common practise, nor would it be possible now-a-days to find a shebeener whose average Sunday takings amounted to £80, as was the case a quarter of a century ago, with a man who carried on a 'business' in Stockwell Street, Glasgow, and whose extensive operations necessitated the employment of a staff of assistants.[7]

The only 'magic' thing about many so-called medicines was the volume of alcohol and other intoxicants they contained. A trade mark dating to 1877. (*Mitchell Library*).

Illicit liquor was BIG business.

The Pharmaceutical Journal highlighted the link between whisky and druggists in a rather amusing anecdote which appeared in its pages in

1867 – 'Latterly these low "druggists" have, in addition to their usual surreptitious Sunday dram-trade, been doing an enormous business in "cholera mixtures," the panacea being of course the whisky.'[8] The article went on to describe how the police had been determined to capture one of the most notorious of these 'druggist-shebeeners', and had sent a detective in plain clothes to ask for a dose of the mixture on a Sunday. The druggist, however, sensed that something was afoot and added a few drops of croton oil (a powerful purgative) to the glass immediately before serving the officer, who waited in eager anticipation to taste the evidence – a necessary task which was regarded as a perk. What happened then became common knowledge throughout the force, the unfortunate man's subsequent embarrassment acting as a lesson to all on how *not* to collect evidence.

'Whisky' and Ether in Ireland

The Irish were no different to the rest of the world when it came to tampering with this and that, and in many respects the adulteration of their whisky (more commonly written as 'whiskey') bore many resemblances to the situation in Glasgow. In 1872 a sample from a public house was analysed by a Doctor Hodges and found to contain a large amount of naphtha. Previous samples analysed by the same man had revealed substances like copper sulphate, cayenne pepper, and sulphuric acid, one particular whisky – said to be a 'fair specimen of the drink sold in low-class public houses' – being made entirely of naphtha, with a slight colouring of whisky.[9] The headline 'Methylated Whiskey' was used to cover the story in *The Pharmaceutical Journal*.

In another example published in *The Chemist and Druggist*, Lord Dunboyne, a magistrate on the bench at the Ennis Licensing Sessions, heard a confession from an ex-publican in which he said that he never expected to go to heaven because he had poisoned so many people. When working in the trade he used to make fourteen quarts of 'pure whisky' by mixing one quart of whisky with one of vitriol, and adding water to make the required volume. The final mixture was, according to the *British Pharmacopoeia*, whisky and dilute sulphuric acid. Lord Dunboyne was thought to be a trifle gullible for believing the story, but there is no doubt that it was based on fact.[10]

As far as druggists are concerned, those in Ireland were every bit as devious as their counterparts across the water; indeed some were performing alchemic ruses reminiscent of the biblical water-into-wine saga. In June 1871 *The Food Journal* reported the antics of one 'itenerant quack' who mixed up naphtha, cayenne pepper, sulphuric acid, blue-stone (copper sulphate), and spirits of wine to convert 'a gallon of water into a gallon of whisky at the cost of one penny.'[11]

To some of our Celtic cousins the risks involved in drinking public house 'whisky' were too great, and many turned to methylated spirits-based ether for their gratification. In Draperstown, County Derry, consumption of this new beverage became so prevalent that sales of opium declined and druggists became used to people coming into their shop to ask for a glass, in much the same way as they would ordinarily have obtained their whisky or laudanum. The ether was cheaper than whisky, was much less likely to give a severe hangover, and acted very rapidly upon the system, the inebriate being kept fairly intoxicated with four or five doses a day.[12]

Before its use in Ireland was made public, the drinking of ether had only occasionally been referred to in the press, most examples having a medical background where it was employed to alleviate pain. One gentleman was known to take about two ounce each day for the relief of asthma; another drank a pint a day to dull the intense pain he suffered as a result of intestinal inflammation. It was also thought that women 'of the higher ranks of society' used ether as a stimulant, and between that and Eau de Cologne – which was also said to be drank by some – certain Victorian ladies must have smelt very peculiar.

The practice of ether drinking in Ireland in the 1860/70s was practically confined to the areas of Londonderry, Antrim, and Tyrone, and in these counties its use had no 'parallel in the history of narcotic stimulants.' Belfast was the main depot which received supplied from manufacturers in Glasgow, Edinburgh, and Dublin, and despatched consignments to the smaller towns. One reason put forward at the time to account for ether's popularity was that the Roman Catholic clergy were driving their flock away from whisky, unknowingly into the clutches of yet another evil. The fact that most consumers were Catholic seems to have given credence to the theory.

Ether was usually drunk neat, the normal method being to take a mouthful of water before, and another after. The drinker would then become rapidly intoxicated, evidence of his strange habit filling the air all around him.

I am credibly informed that at the fair of Draperstown – which appears to be the paradise of ether drinkers – the prevalent smell is not, as at country fairs, of pigs, tobacco-smoke, or of unwashed human beings, but of ether.[13]

A Notorious Glasgow Druggist

The Glasgow Post Office Directory for 1867/68 lists Joseph Clark as a druggist and surgeon at 38 Saltmarket and 33 Kent Street, Glasgow; his house at 16 South St. Mungo Street.

Saltmarket was a bustling thoroughfare leading from the Cross, whose dark and narrow closes and wynds were densely overcrowded with the poorer inhabitants of the city. A variety of traders carried out their business in shops in the street, and these included eating-houses, victuallers, oyster-rooms, tobacconists, undertakers, and a rather large number of spirit merchants. Work was taking place to demolish some of the worst buildings and to generally improve the whole sanitary environment, but it was only partially under way and for many residents the only escape was to be found at the bottom of a bottle.

Come Sundays, the public houses were closed, and on this day of rest Joseph Clark did a roaring trade. In one week he was known to have sold fifty-three gallons of 'finish', a feat which was eventually brought to the attention of the authorities.

On the 27th October 1867 an Excise Officer entered Clark's shop and purchased a Seidlitz powder (a saline aperient). While it was being mixed, the officer asked for a glass of 'finish' to take with it, to which Clark replied that he would have to take it outside to drink. Half-a-gill was duly paid for and removed from the premises, and on analysis was found to consist of the expected methylated spirits and gum. The case was brought to court.

Mr J. L. Lang, appearing for the defence, said that Clark's shop was situated in a neighbourhood where there were many hatters and polishers, and it was to them that the 'finish' was supplied for use in their trade. Also, Clark had written to the Inland Revenue to ask for clarification on certain points raised in an order issued to all druggists regarding the sale of 'finish', but no reply had been received. Unfortunately, Clark could not name one person or business to whom he had made sales for legitimate use, and this, combined with the fact that when the officer made the purchase he had said that it was for drinking, meant that 'Guilty' was the only verdict. A mitigated penalty of £30 was imposed.[14]

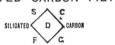
A page from *The Chemist and Druggist* of October 1879 showing a few of the many firms who supplied alcohol to retail druggists. It was usually the warming glow of spirit intoxication that convinced members of the public that a particular medicine was of some worth. (*Mitchell Library*).

The drinking of 'finish' was a problem that continued for many years. In 1887 druggists in Edinburgh were becoming increasingly concerned with the large numbers of poor people who were drinking methylated spirits. One retailer whose letter appeared in *The Scottish Wine, Spirit, and Beer Trades' Review* told of having 'little difficulty in discriminating between the *bona-fide* polisher, etc., and the would-be imbiber of this poison.'[15] The use of the word 'polisher' indicates that the writer was probably referring to 'finish', as opposed to methylated spirits, and this perhaps adds weight to the previously-mentioned confusion that existed between the two similar liquids. In Dumfries in 1888 there were at least three druggists who sold 'finish' for drinking purposes on Sundays. More than a gallon of the stuff could be sold in just over an hour, and at a profit of 5s per gallon a tremendous potential existed for making a lot of money. One shop in the town used to take eight gallons a week from a firm in Glasgow and realise a profit of £2 from this alone.[16] Joseph Clark must have been making a fortune back in 1867.

Clark's case was mentioned in the *North British Daily Mail's* 1872 whisky disclosure. It was given as evidence of the fact that 'finish' was indeed drunk in Glasgow, and in no small measure. Its use among the lower classes was widespread and there was really no good reason why it shouldn't be one of many substances employed to adulterate the poor man's tipple.

Up to this point in our examination of the strange goings-on in Glasgow, it has been assumed that the shellac element of 'finish' was an undesirable and useless substance which the fraudulent spirit dealer could well have done without; it was the methylated spirits that he wanted, as a substitute for the more-costly whisky. Druggists who retailed 'finish' to avoid having to pay the methylated spirits licence, and who sometimes sold it with less than the required amount of shellac, were, it might be thought, regularly patronised by those who dealt in adulterated spirits. However, a letter which appeared in the 'Mail directly after Professor Anderson's effort, exploded this notion and put shellac in a very different light. Far from being an extraneous material of little benefit in the adulteration of whisky, its role was to give the much-diluted spirit a bit of colour. Lac – the basic form of shellac – is a dark red hue, and when combined with other coloured adulterants would have imparted a very rough whisky-like tinge.

Some shebeeners were not exactly adept at getting the colour blend right. In the 'Mail's report, whisky sample No.17 was 'a peculiar pinkish yellow', No.21 was 'clear and limpid, with a very faint pink tinge', and No.27 was a nightmarish 'pinkish green'. Shellac was detected by Doctor Gray in all three, No.27 having a 'large quantitie', and made entirely from 'finish' and water. While the observed pink tint is probably due to the presence of shellac, it is of some interest to briefly mention that one or two samples contained it but were clear in colour. Presumably this is simply because of a much smaller quantity of shellac and a lack of skill by the mixer in obtaining a good colour balance. No.5, for example, was a public house whisky; it had 60 grains of shellac per gallon (a very small amount) and had no colour. No.15 (a shebeen whisky) was also colourless, and contained sheellac along with turpentine and other unimaginables. Of course in some of the dingiest drinking-dens it wouldn't have mattered what the colour was. Poor quality gas-lighting or candles, combined with the drinker's intoxicated condition, meant that 'whisky' could have been blue and still drunk with relish!

The letter writer who divulged the information with regard to shellac signed himself 'A Citizen' from Hillhead, but the content and sources referred to in his letter reveals him to be a well-read man whose access to periodicals like *The Pharmaceutical Journal* points to him being a doctor or scientist, possibly linked in some way with Glasgow University, who, for whatever reason, did not wish to make himself known.[17]

He also set the record straight on the definition of 'finish', and went on to say that shellac could be dissolved in other solvents apart from methylated spirits; for example, in naphtha. This is a refreshing breath of air in the whole controversy. Methylated spirits-based 'finish' was the most popular version of this fine varnish, but to have it verified that other solvents might be used throws a bit of a damper on the fire of Doctor Gray's critics and helps to explain the mention of Berlin spirit in the analysis. Nevertheless, it is difficult to understand why Berlin spirit (even in an impure and fraudulently imported form) would be used instead of the presumably more-readily available and cheaper methylated spirits, and we have to retain some cautious uncertainties about this aspect of the results. There were others who were more sceptical, as we shall see later.

The final word in this chapter rests with 'A Citizen.'

There cannot be a doubt that water is the chief adulterant, for the obvious reason that an increase of the saleable quantity of the liquid is what is sought by the vendor, be he distiller, wholesale dealer, or retailer, and water is the cheapest and readiest material for the purpose. But dilution of the spirit by water has its limit, and to extend that limit by giving pungency and "bite" to the spirit through other and chemical adulterants is the aim of the dishonest dealer.

6

Analysts Never Agree

ON the 16th October, three weeks after the *North British Daily Mail's* whisky story broke, Doctor James St. Clair Gray put pen to paper to defend his analytical results, and his good name, against the insinuated charges of incompetence levelled at him by Professor Anderson. His letter was published in the 'Mail the next day.

As we have already seen, Anderson's letter itself was riddled with errors and inaccuracies and Doctor Gray pointed these out, often making reference to previous correspondence from members of the public to put the learned professor in his place. He also described the various tests he had used to detect the adulterants, and this, bearing in mind that his letter was for insertion in a daily newspaper and not some scientific journal, he did with moderate detail. It was important for him to demonstrate how he had found methyl alcohol, when present in a mixture with ethyl alcohol, as, in the eyes of many chemists, this was an impossibility.

> As to the process employed for the detection of methylic alcohol – By distillation at a temperature rather under 160 deg. Fah., a small portion of an alcoholic liquid was obtained in the receiver, possessing the odour of methylic alcohol, burning with a clear blue flame, and giving with powdered caustic potash a brown colouration almost immediately on the addition of the reagent.

The presence of turpentine was confirmed by a test that was so sensitive that he was able to detect ten drops in a gallon of spirit. In addition, its 'well known odour' had been apparent. Other tests were listed for amyl alcohol, shellac, sulphuric acid, 'a salt of copper', hydrochloric acid, and zinc.

It may be thought that too much reliance was placed upon ability to smell certain substances, but this was only one of a number of methods the scientist used to confirm the identity of a material under scrutiny. The analyst 'could not trust any one test' and 'was encouraged to carry out as many as possible.' Back in 1855 when Professors Graham, Hofmann, and Redwood were inventing methylated spirits, their report stated that the characteristic and persistent odour of methylic spirit was not difficult to detect, even when highly diluted.

Doctor Gray had learned how important a sense of smell was when he assisted Professor Harry Rainy with forensic cases at Glasgow University in the late 1860s. At that time one of the traditional methods of detecting poisons was by the distinctive odour they gave off when boiled. Indeed, such was the rudimentary state of analytical chemistry that in the search for opium or strychnine in a corpse thought to have been poisoned, the analyst was expected to 'taste the boiled-down extracts of bodily organs.'[1]

On the subject of copper and zinc, Professor Anderson could not understand why the salts of these metals should be used as they imparted a 'disgusting metallic flavour.' Again, Doctor Gray put him right. He referred to Arthur Hassall's 1855 book, *Food and its Adulterations*, in which, at page 642, it is stated that zinc sulphate was probably used to clarify adulterated gin. As far as copper was concerned, the *Boston Medical and Surgical Journal* of 7th September 1860 was quoted.

> Newly-distilled spirits, of the most common kind, often contain salts of copper, of lead, or tin, derived from the condensers, in which the vapours are reduced to a fluid form. The quantity of copper salt contained in the bulk usually taken as a draught is sufficient to produce the minor effects of metallic poisoning; the cumulative character of these poisons may even lead to fatal consequences.

The *'Mail's* shebeen sample No. 15 had a 'sweetish disagreeable metallic taste' and was found to contain copper and iron. Public house sample No. 11 also contained a copper salt and had a 'pungent metallic and alcoholic' taste. This peculiar metallic property evidently did not put people off drinking the whisky, although such rot-gut spirit would have been swiftly washed down with beer (which was probably also adulterated) to rid the mouth of any lingering tang.

Having seen off the bulk of Anderson's criticisms, Gray then agreed

109

to submit the remainder of his samples for analysis by a 'neutral chemist of standing', as proposed by William Smyth, Secretary of the Glasgow Wine, Spirit, and Beer Trade Association. Robert R. Tatlock was the chemist Mr Smyth had in mind, but unfortunately the 'Mail would not authorise Doctor Gray to hand over the samples to him. Smyth then wrote to the 'Mail to ask if they would allow any other analytical chemist to carry out tests on the remaining whisky, and if so, who.

From this moment onwards the arguments become decidedly heated. In order to give you a feel of how these developed, and to allow a glimpse of the seriousness with which the whisky report was quite rightly viewed, I think it is only fair that I quote the next two letters in full. The whole of the Scottish spirit industry waited with bated breath as each day's *North British Daily Mail* hit the streets …

> The Editor of the *Mail* has to acknowledge Mr Smyth's letter of yesterday, and will have much pleasure, as he proposes, in handing over the remainders of the samples analysed by Dr Gray to any neutral chemist of high standing. In reply to Mr Smyth's suggestion that he should name such a chemist, the Editor would suggest Dr Charles A. Cameron, public analyst for the county and city of Dublin, as the public analyst of longest standing in the United Kingdom. It may be well to mention that Dr Cameron is in no way related to the person of the same name connected with the *Mail*, and that the slight acquaintance which exists between them originated in the inadvertent opening of each other's letters while stopping at the same London hotel. As was explained in the second article, the samples submitted to Dr Gray for analysis were small, the directions to those employed in collecting them being to obtain them as they were ordinarily retailed. They were, therefore, in great part, consumed in the process of examination. The remainders are so small, and have been so much exposed to the atmosphere to render any results concerning the volatile alcohols which they may yield of little value. They should, however, amply suffice to enable the chemist to determine the presence of non-volatile substances, such as sulphuric acid, copper, zinc, and shellac, if not all in one specimen, at least one in one and another in another, and the presence or absence of these will practically determine the presence or absence of those forms of adulteration about which there has been any question. As Mr Smyth speaks of thirty specimens, the Editor presumes it is desired to test the shebeen as well as the public house samples. The shebeen samples were almost entirely obtained through the kindness of

the police, who had effected their capture, so that there should be no difficulty in obtaining from the same source as many more samples as may be deemed advisable, which, if not identical with those examined by Dr Gray, should be sufficiently similar for all practical purposes to establish or disprove the accuracy of his analyses.[2]

Doctor Cameron, Dublin's public analyst, was a wise choice. The adulteration of whisky in Ireland was reasonably well-documented in the mid-Victorian period, as we have already seen, and much experience had obviously been gained in testing whisky whose illegitimate contents were more than similar to those found in Glasgow. Further proof that Cameron was indeed closely linked with the analysis of whisky is found in the Government's 1890 Report on *British and Foreign Spirits*, in which he is mentioned as giving evidence before the 'Committee on the Adulteration of Foods Act in 1872, on the question of fusel oil.' During his public duties he had taken samples of thousands of whiskies, and it was a subject he was 'peculiarly well up in.'

The Glasgow Wine, Spirit, and Beer Trade Association were far from happy. Their letter, from the secretary, William Smyth, to the *'Mail's* editor, was published on the 19th October.

Sir, – In reply to yours of 16th, it is to be regretted beyond measure that such carelessness has been displayed with regard to the samples. It seems incredible that so much noise has been made, involving irreparable mischief to innocent dealers, and that the accusers have for ever deprived the public of the only means of disproving the assertions made, by failing to produce the samples in the state in which they were said to be purchased. We are now coolly told that any results as regards the alcohols which another chemist may find will not be of much service, as the samples have been rendered useless, as far as these ingredients go, by their having been exposed to the air. We are thus for ever deprived of the means of corroborative evidence as to the alleged presence of methylated spirit and fousel oil; and we are further informed that another chemist need not be expected to detect all the ingredients, but only one in one sample and another in another. What would be thought of the qualifications of an ordinary analytical chemist who could not produce on being required to do so, the samples he had drawn and analysed without saying that he had allowed them to spoil, and that the principal ingredients which were the subject of dispute could not longer be detected? The samples could have been kept with ease in their original state simply by placing them in bottles, and why this was not

done it is impossible to surmise. This is another example of the loose manner in which the whole matter has been gone about from first to last, and which we shall shortly have occasion sufficiently to show. We have been deprived of any alternative but to allow the destroyed samples to go to another chemist; but why take them to Dublin? Is not Glasgow the Scottish centre of chemical manufactures, and are there not more analytical chemists of standing and first-class practice, with long years' experience here, than elsewhere in the United Kingdom, perhaps not even excepting London? One reason may be that we do not believe there is one public chemist in Glasgow who would believe a tenth part of the romancing contained in your report headed "Mysteries of Glasgow Whisky," and which are due in most part to the lively imagination of a non-professional chemist. We can only consent to Dr Cameron of Dublin receiving the remainder of the spoiled samples for analysis on the understanding that another chemist on behalf of this association receives one-half of each also. No sample is so small that it cannot be divided, and both chemists would have an equal chance. I may add, that it is not our intention to have anything to do with the alleged shebeen samples, and you are in error in stating that I mentioned "thirty" specimens. We are only interested in the ordinary public house samples, which you state were collected as they were ordinarily retailed.
WILL. SMYTH.
144 Queen Street, Glasgow.

This was fighting talk. You can just imagine the gasp of disbelief that emanated from Doctor Gray's frame as he pored over his newspapers during breakfast. Here was some buffoon accusing him of being a non-professional chemist with a 'lively imagination'. Not only that, but he was insinuating that the samples may have been interfered with to give results that were false. Doctor Gray could hardly fail to be roused to anger.

If there was every any chance of obtaining a confirmatory analysis, then Smyth's conditions now made that practically impossible. What did he have to fear from Dublin's analyst? – The truth? If we consider this question, then we must also consider why the 'Mail refused to let Robert R. Tatlock near the samples. Was the 'Mail frightened of gross inaccuracies in the results, or was the situation as hinted in an earlier court-case we examined where it was said that 'scientific men could always take a scientific view according to the wishes of the party whose cause they were engaged to support; and science was not yet so certain but that they might do so conscientiously.' In other words, could Gray have concocted results to fit a verbal prompting given by the 'Mail's editor? Might Tatlock have obtained his own set of results which would have been looked on favourably by Mr Smyth? Neither scenario appears likely. Science was not yet at that definite stage where one thing is right and another wrong. Analysts might have found themselves on either side of the fence as far as the whisky tests are concerned, and still have been essentially correct. One man says he can detect methyl alcohol, the other says he cannot; it was all over, bar for the shouting.

Charles Cameron, the 'Mail's editor, was certainly on the verge of shouting. He must have been incensed, along with a great many other people, with Smyth's cutting and slanderous remarks. His reply to Smyth also appeared in the newspaper on October 19th, and there was now no-holds-barred. He first of all assured him that the remaining whisky samples were in reasonable condition and that twelve of those from public houses were still housed in their original bottles, all corked, sealed, and labelled. He mentioned the 'inexcusably discourteous' passages in Smyth's letter, and went on to say that Dublin's analyst was the most experienced in the United Kingdom. Had this choice for a second analyst been restricted to Glasgow, the editor 'could not have been so unjust to Dr Gray as to ask him to submit his results to any but a chemist of higher official status than himself, and the Professor of Chemistry in the University, who alone possessed that qualification, had already disqualified himself for the position of umpire, by a publication on the subject with which Dr Gray has, the Editor thinks, very satisfactorily dealt.' He then explained exactly what he had meant, in his previous letter, with regard to the condition of the samples and their alcohol content.

Had not the Editor been willing to afford the fullest facility for a fair and candid investigation of the matter, he would not have thought it necessary to volunteer the information which was not unlikely to escape persons unacquainted with chemical operations, that small quantities of spirits exposed to the heated atmosphere of a laboratory, and necessarily occasionally uncorked, would probably be found to have parted with their more volatile constituents to such an extent as in some measure to interfere with the value of any results now obtainable concerning these. But to any unprejudiced chemist the presence of shellac, for example, in the residue of a sample said to have contained methylic alcohol, would, even should the latter fail to be now detectible, afford the strongest possible presumptive proof of its original presence.

The editor was talking about the presence of 'finish' (methylated spirits and shellac), and one has to admit that what he says makes a lot of sense.

On Smyth's comments regarding the doubtful purchase of the samples and the innuendo of falsification, the editor stated that he could prove that the samples were purchased as described, but if this was still doubted then it was pointless carrying on with further tests.

Were every discovery of Dr Gray's confirmed ten times over, and were the identity of each original sample procured indisputably proved, it might equally well consist with Mr Smyth's notions of courtesy and candour to insinuate that Dr Gray had tampered with the residues previously to sealing them up; and therefore the Editor must decline to waste any more time, or to expose himself to any more insult, by further correspondence with Mr Smyth on the subject.

Of course it was now just over three weeks since the first whisky report, and publicans in Glasgow would have been more than interested in the increasingly intense arguments that were taking place in the '*Mail*. It must have been obvious that the whole shebang was gradually heading towards a crisis which could only be alleviated by the taking of further samples. Any publican who had previously added methylated spirits to his whisky, or any of the other alleged ingredients, (and remember, this practice was confined to a proportion of the less-respectable howffs – not them all) would have ceased forthwith in anticipation of a visit from someone in authority. It was, therefore, now impossible to repeat the tests on fresh samples, hence why so much importance was attached to the residues of the original whisky.

Greenock is Dragged into the Debate
Professor Anderson, no doubt wishing to join in the tirade of abuse that was being thrown at Doctor Gray, waded once more into the thick of things on October 21st. He found it quite absurd that methyl alcohol was detected by smell, and regarded many of Gray's other tests as defective. He highly approved of the proposition to have the

Professor Thomas Anderson, c1870. (*Glasgow University Archives*).

remaining samples examined by another chemist, but instead of Dublin's Doctor Cameron he recommended a Doctor Frankland or Doctor Odling.

Taking issue with the correspondent 'Nicol Jarvie', he was adamant that he was correct with regard to the amount of methyl alcohol in wood spirit – 'It rarely exceeds 20 or 30 per cent.' Once again, Anderson was wrong. Around 70 per cent was the usual figure for the amount of methyl alcohol contained in the purified naphtha used in making methylated spirits. For it to contain 20 or 30 per cent, it would have to be at an early stage of its distillation, and would be termed pyroligneous acid, or 'crude wood vinegar', and not naphtha proper.

The *Greenock Telegraph* then became involved. In its edition of 19th April 1871, results were given of the analysis of thirty-six samples of whisky. Anderson pointed out that no adulteration had been found other than that with water, even although methyl alcohol and other substances had been carefully sought after. In his opinion, this merely backed up the notion that the *'Mail's* survey had been wrong from start to finish. If Glasgow's whisky was so tainted, then surely Greenock's should be also? What he failed to say is that wood spirit *had* been detected in two of the Greenock samples, although it was found in such minute quantities that it was doubtful whether adulteration had taken place. Considering the difficulty that existed in the early 1870s in detecting wood spirit, or naphtha, when in the presence of ethyl, or 'ordinary', alcohol, I should say that the finding of even a small amount of wood spirit was significant. Professor Anderson didn't seem to think so.

By October 21st, the *'Mail's* editor had come to the conclusion that enough was enough. No more could be gained by prolonging the debate, which was turning out to be one of his more troublesome pieces. To bring the controversy to a close, he handed a pile of letters to Doctor Gray and asked him to reply so that his answer could be published simultaneously. Doctor Gray, who had much more to do with his time than to enter into discussion with the likes of Professor Anderson, complied. Besides, he really had no choice – his career and reputation were now on the line.

He described how he had himself analysed some twenty-two samples of whisky bought in Greenock, Paisley, and Port Glasgow in the last ten days, and discovered no adulteration other than with water. He defended his finding of methyl alcohol, this time in greater detail than before, and emphasised the importance of smell in detecting something which was employed solely because of its noxious properties.

> As to Methylic Alcohol – The process employed was that known as Ure's process, and concerning this process, the following paragraph will be found in "Muspratt's Chemistry," page 146: –
> "Dr Ure says that caustic potassa in powder is the most delicate test for the detection of wood spirit in alcohol; for if wood spirit is present the liquor assumes then a brown colour, while pulverised potassa does not alter the colour of pure alcohol, even after several hours; and it is only after a whole day's contact that a feeble yellowish tinge is then developed. But if the alcohol contains only two per cent, or even one per cent of wood spirit, it turns yellowish in the course of ten minutes, and brown in half an hour."

I think even a layman can see that Doctor Gray's means of discovering methyl alcohol was fairly straightforward and logical. It appears to offer conclusive proof of the presence of methyl alcohol in a mixture with ethyl alcohol. So, one might ask, what was all the fuss about?

Details were given of the other tests that were conducted, each note bearing the original reference source from which the test was taken. Gray had not treated the whisky analysis lightly. His sources included *Miller's Chemistry*, *Medical Jurisprudence* by Doctor Alfred Swayne Taylor, *Forensic Medicine* by Doctor Guy, *Adulteration of Food* by Hassall (1855 edition), *Taylor's Medical Jurisprudence*, and Brand and Taylor's *Chemistry*.

Gray had no objection to Anderson's recommendation that the residues be submitted to either Doctor Frankland or Doctor Odling, but reminded him that no one had asked for his recommendation on this matter. He took great offence at some of Anderson's remarks, and one has to wonder at the amount of electricity that might have filled the air whenever they inadvertently passed each other in the cloisters of the building in which they both carried out research.

On the subject of fusel-oil and a previous letter from William Wallace (an analytical chemist who worked with Robert Tatlock), Gray disagreed with the chemist's findings. In Wallace's opinion, as a result of a number of experiments he carried out, fusel-oil mixed with alcohol, in the proportion of one part of the former to 2000 of the latter, renders the mixture practically undrinkable due to the 'extreme

117

rankness of the flavour.' In other words, it is most unlikely that fusel-oil would be used as an adulterant. However, Gray had conducted his own tests ....

> I happen to have also experimented in the matter, and found that a mixture of proof spirit, with about a twentieth part fousel oil – though very unpleasant certainly, was not by any means undrinkable. I did not venture to swallow more than a couple of teaspoonfuls of the mixture myself, but should say that to the indurated palate of the regular dram-drinker the decided "bite" might appear anything but a disadvantage.

The Mystery Continues

If the *'Mail's* editor thought that his hints about ending the controversy following Doctor Gray's 'final' letter would have had any impact, he couldn't have been more wrong. It was now October 23rd, and still letters flooded the newspaper's offices, much to the presumed chagrin of those involved. Many of their special reports had illicited a public response, but none quite like this. The whole thing was running away with itself. The point they had tackled was, indeed, a sore one. Whisky was always a topic with which great passion was associated, and while the adulteration of food and drink was widely known, the adulteration of whisky was something that some people just couldn't grasp; it clawed at the very heart of Scotland.

Three letters appeared on the 23rd. One from 'Nicol Jarvie' who had another dig at Professor Anderson regarding naphtha, one from 'A Dealer' who saw flaws in Doctor Gray's figures with regard to the strength of some samples, and one very detailed letter from someone known simply as 'J.S.' With the tendency for correspondents to receive much flak following the publication of their letter, it is hardly surprising that one or two wished to keep their identity a secret.

The letter from 'J.S.' was no run-of-the-mill offering, the questions he raised and the manner in which they were dealt pointing towards a scientist who had indepth knowledge in the field of chemistry. Chemistry was considered to be an exact science, and as such he would deal with Doctor Gray's report 'principally on scientific grounds', as the report itself was a scientific investigation. He accused Doctor Gray of being 'rather vague' in his descriptive terminology, and backed 'A Dealer' in finding much at fault with his figures.

As no less eminent a chemist than Dr Anderson did not understand, I may be pardoned if I cannot comprehend these "discrepancies" which are not "slight," but so very great as to destroy all faith in the correctness of Dr Gray's analyses.

The report by Professors Graham, Hoffman, and Redwood which examined the viability of methylated spirits was then mentioned. In it, the difficulties in separating methyl alcohol were confronted and put forward as a good reason for using it in a mixture with spirits of wine. If it was difficult to separate, then there was less chance of removing the methyl portion to attain a cheap, illicit and drinkable spirit. If these renowned professors could not isolate methyl alcohol, then how on earth could Doctor Gray determine its presence?

Had Dr Gray confined himself to saying he found this characteristic odour and taste it might be understood, but he seeks to confirm this, and gives a chemical tests as a conclusive one which in reality has no value.

To demonstrate the uselessness of Gray's test for methyl alcohol, 'J.S.' quoted the above professors ....

Lastly, a few experiments were made with the view of establishing the presence of methylic spirit in alcoholic mixtures by the dark yellowish brown colour wood-spirit assumes when left in contact with either solid hydrate of potash or soda. But it was found that the brown colour assumed by methylic spirit was only little more intense than that which alcohol shows when similarly treated.

To the casual reader, both in Victorian times and today, the chemical side of things must seem very complicated. However, I make no apologies. I have omitted the bulk of the scientific data that accompanied each day's articles or letters, and only include the most crucial elements to give you an idea of the intricacy and rate of progression of the arguments as a whole. Should you have an interest in chemistry or the unedited picture of Glasgow's spirituous mystery, then by all means please refer to the *North British Daily Mail.*

There were, thankfully, still those around who were defending Doctor Gray. One, whose letter appeared on the 25th October, reviewed the complete saga in plain and simple language so as to inform and remind

119

the casual reader of exactly what had taken place in the preceding month. Such a well-structured letter of immense common sense can only be quoted in full and will allow us to step back for a breather and recap.

Sir, – I hope you will not close the correspondence on this subject at a moment when the point in dispute is not clearly before the public mind, for I observe that your critical correspondents have (no doubt quite unintentionally) turned the discussion to matters entirely irrelevant. Yet the issue is very simple, and lies wholly in this question – Were or were not these foreign substances present which Dr St. Clair Gray affirms he detected in the samples of whisky you submitted to him for analysis? It is very clear that this question can neither be answered by wrangles as to the quantity of any adulterant (such as fousel oil) that may chance to be in the market, nor by speculating on the possible reasons for using one or other of these substances. Least of all, can it be answered by asserting the comparative purity of *other samples altogether*, bought, too, in the very crisis of the alarm produced in the spirit trade by your revelations. In short, it is manifest that Dr Gray's statements can only be met by a direct and explicit denial of their truth; and, since it does not appear that his most vehement critics venture to impugn his personal veracity, this denial must rest either on an alleged defect in the methods of analysis employed by him, or an alleged incapacity on his part to use those methods rightly. The latter point will be settled to a certain extent by the analysis of the remaining samples, which is about to be undertaken by some neutral person, and it can be settled in no other way; but Dr Gray's results receive confirmation from the fact that he discovered no kind of adulteration which had not been discovered before, for every substance detected by him will be found enumerated (along with some others) in Hassall's or any other good work on adulteration. There remains, therefore, for discussion, only the trustworthiness of Dr Gray's methods – a point which has been touched on by Dr T. Anderson alone, of all your correspondents. It is, of course, impossibly to handle such a matter technically in your columns; but I think it will be easy, nevertheless, to give your readers some solid grounds for a definite opinion respecting it. Dr Anderson's letters have elicited from Dr Gray a complete account of his processes and the authorities for them, and after perusing this account Dr Anderson declares his doubts of the results to be "materially strengthened;" he characterises the test for methyl as one "on which no chemist of experience would for a moment rely;" that for amylic alcohol he calls

120

"defective," and that for turpentine "still more doubtful." Now, though I am not without some fondness for chemistry myself, and, I think, some knowledge of it, I have taken the precaution to verify nearly the whole of Dr Gray's references, and have found them to be correct. I have found that in all he did he was supported by the authority of such men as Ure, Miller, Muspratt, Deville, Taylor, and others, who form, without exception, the most distinguished and the safest guides any chemist can follow, and whose names and reputation must insure the confidence of every intelligent reader, whether he have any special acquaintance with their science or not. It is against the accumulated weight of these authorities that Dr T. Anderson, interposing, delivers his dictum, and stranger still, finds his doubts confirmed by detailed descriptions of the operations, which must have at once told any chemist the authority on which they rested. This dispute therefore is now narrowed to a conflict of opinion, on which Dr T. Anderson takes one side, and the whole world of chemists have taken the other. I wish to speak with the greatest possible respect of Dr T. Anderson, nor could anything have been more repugnant to me than a criticism of the doctor's professional status as a chemist. But he has chosen voluntarily to take up a position in which, as I have shown, he pits the influence of his own opinion against that of the most trusted teachers of the science, and I think we should fail in our duty to their fame if this position were left undisputed. Dr Anderson may be a very competent chemist, but I do him no wrong when I affirm that he is not an eminent one. I am not unfamiliar with the literature and history of chemistry, yet in all the records of the science I do not recollect ever to have seen the name of Dr Anderson once mentioned; and were it not that the fact of his official position is accidentally within my knowledge, I should never, as a student of chemistry, have been able to guess that Dr Anderson had for twenty years sat in the chair once filled by Black and Cullen. This is a disagreeable matter to enlarge upon, and I shall content myself with having spoken the plain truth, and leave my words to be justified by the knowledge of every man who reads them. I shall only repeat then that all the pertinent criticisms of the charges of adulteration brought against the spirit trade in your journal resolve themselves into a wholesale condemnation by Dr T. Anderson, of all the methods of analysis adopted by the most famous chemists of this and other countries, and followed by your analyst. Does a man need to be a chemist to judge the value of such criticism. It is chance alone which had brought this correspondence under my notice. Entirely unconnected with Glasgow, or with trade of any kind whatever, I write only in the interest of science, and to do the little I can to keep the real question in the public mind. I have addressed myself exclusively to the

general reader, who is most concerned and who must judge for himself in this matter; but I may be permitted, under the shelter of the anonymous, to sign myself, Sir, – Yours, etc.,
AN OXFORD FIRST CLASS MAN IN NATURAL SCIENCE, London, Oct. 23.[3]

Tatlock and the Glasgow Herald

Robert Rattray Tatlock was born in Glasgow in the year of Queen Victoria's Coronation in 1837. His father was a hat manufacturer in Argyle Street in the 1830s; no doubt one who used legally-gotten spirituous solvents in his varnishes. As a young man, Robert was educated at Greyfriars' School in Shuttle Street – a building which, at that time, was roofed with thatch – and then moved to the Trades House School where he found an interest in chemistry under the enthusiastic teachings of the superintendent, Mr Struthers. Such was his liking for this science that he attended evening classes at Anderson's College. Professor Penny, the tutor at Anderson's, must have glimpsed great keenness and potential in Tatlock's work, and consequently employed him as his sole assistant for the next ten years. In 1867 he set himself up in business as an analytical chemist and by 1872 was resident in his Analytical Laboratory at 42 Bath Street, as part of the firm Wallace, Tatlock & Clark.[4] It was not long after the whisky disclosure that the three members of this company became public analysts for the city of Glasgow.

As we have already seen, Tatlock was initially approached by the secretary of the Glasgow Wine, Spirit, and Beer Trade Association on October 15th in connection with obtaining the whisky residues for a confirmatory analysis, but Dr Gray had been instructed not to hand over the samples. Mr Smyth, the above secretary, then asked Tatlock for a report, in the absence of the samples, on the written analysis as published in the pages of the 'Mail, and, sensing that he might have no joy with publication in the 'Mail, sent the complete report to the *Glasgow Herald*.

On Friday and Saturday, the 25th and 26th October 1872, Tatlock's lengthy article was printed. Under the title CHEMICAL REPORT ON "THE MYSTERIES OF GLASGOW WHISKY", he really went to town on Doctor Gray's analysis, finding something wrong with practically every test he used. Starting with the condition of the samples, he expressed his opinion that whoever had taken them was certainly no analytical chemist as the volume collected should have been large enough to allow duplicates to be retained and sealed for any future inspection.

Gray's use of Ure's process for detecting methylic spirit was, in Tatlock's eyes, useless, and harked back to the days when 'organic chemistry could hardly be said to exist.' Turpentine fared no better. The 'dark red viscous mass' that Gray's test produced was probably due to the presence of sugar – not turpentine. Every test was defective.

> ... I am clearly of the opinion that many of the averments made cannot be supported, that substances are named as having been found in the samples which, in presence of the other ingredients said to have been found, it would be utterly impossible for any chemist to detect.

Tatlock was not a man to mince his words. A letter later appeared in the 'Mail on October 29th in connection with the above statement. If, as was suggested, it was impossible for any chemist to detect the adulterants said to have been found in Glasgow's whisky, then surely publicans could adulterate with impunity? Such words of wisdom would have done little to restore the confidence of citizens whose view of their local spirit merchants had been dealt a severe blow.

According to Tatlock, the 'Mail's disclosure that out of fourteen samples of public house whisky sold in Glasgow, six contained methyl alcohol, was quite incredible. That such a large proportion should make use of a spirit that 'could not be obtained in any great quantity' and thereby put themselves at risk of prosecution was simply unbelievable. Here he fails to grasp the laws surrounding methylated spirits. A gallon could be obtained, as we have already seen, as easily as a gallon of milk, and anyone wishing to amass a reasonably large quantity would have no trouble in making the maximum allowable purchase from any number of druggists. In the case of 'finish' – some of which was sold with no gum, and was therefore just methylated spirits – there was no limit on the amount sold, although care would have to be taken to avoid attracting the sort of attention that Joseph Clark's fifty-three gallons in one week did back in 1867. There is no doubt that methylated spirits *could* be obtained in 'great quantity', and Tatlock was wrong to say otherwise.

You must remember that any publican who *did* use methylated spirits

Robert Rattray Tatlock, as depicted in *The Bailie* in 1898. Tatlock was closely involved with the arguments following the 1872 whisky disclosure, before becoming a long-standing public analyst for the city of Glasgow. (*Mitchell Library*).

did not add it to *all* of his whisky. Such adulterated spirit would have been kept separate from the regular whisky and only served to persons selected by the bar-staff as unlikely to notice the difference, or to complain if they did. It was, therefore, the poorer, indiscriminating classes, or passing travellers, who were served such poison. Locals would know in which cask it was housed and would make doubly certain that none of it came their way, although after a heavy night I'm sure some would have passed their lips unknowingly, the mother-of-all-hangovers being the signal that all was not as it should have been the night before.

Over the following week Tatlock and Gray went at it tooth and nail in the pages of the 'Mail. Each retort was filled with an increasing amount of venom as insult after insult was flung backwards and forwards, much to the presumed amazement of all onlookers. In Gray's immediate answer to Tatlock he was as sure and confident as he had been at the onset, and defended each and every accusation with convincing conviction. Further references were brought into play, and any reader who was still able to understand the complex arguments must have felt great admiration for Gray in the way that he parried all of Tatlock's potentially damaging blows. The people's champion was fighting back.

On the topic of methyl alcohol, Gray stood by Ure's process and reintroduced Professors Graham and Redwood as eminent men who, far from regarding the technique as ineffective, acknowledged its validity and reliability. Gray felt it necessary to remind his adversary that the brown tinge seen in the test was apparent after thirty minutes when as little as one per cent methyl alcohol was mixed with ethyl alcohol, but took twenty-four hours when the spirit was solely ethylic. In other words, while a similar colour was found with ethyl alcohol, the time it took to form that colour was the basis of the test for methyl alcohol.

In the case of turpentine, Gray informed Tatlock that the presence of sugar gives a jet-black coloured mass, and not red, and so production of the latter hue was a correct indicator. Tatlock, it seems, was making just as many slip-ups as any analyst of the period, most not being slip-ups in the true sense of the word, but differences of opinion, or in interpretation, in a convoluted chemical jigsaw. The only concession was of a minor nature, and Gray gave it mockingly …

> One discovery of Mr Tatlock's I admit – that of a typographical error, consisting of the substitution of "oz." for "grs," and this in a position where it was so obvious that even Mr Tatlock cannot attribute it to malevolence or ignorance. This discovery is about the most important result of his month's labours.

Tatlock responded immediately, his letter appearing in the '*Mail* on October 29th. He suggested that the original whisky reports and Gray's reply to Anderson, along with his own report, should be sent to any one of a number of qualified men, the list he provided including such names as Doctor Odling, Professor of Chemistry in the University of Oxford; Doctor Frankland, Professor of Chemistry in the Royal College of Chemistry in London; Doctor Williamson, Professor of Chemistry in University College in London; and Doctor Alex. Crum, Professor of Chemistry in the University of Edinburgh.

Not wishing to prolong such a complex issue in a public newspaper, Tatlock then invited Gray to appear before the Glasgow Philosophical Society to discuss the matter of length. Tatlock was secretary of the chemical section of the society and offered to arrange a special night to suit him at any time over the next six months. Gray was being forced into a corner.

A Declaration

Letters from other interested parties were still being published, including one from 'J.H.' who defended Professor Anderson against the attack from 'An Oxford First Class Man in Natural Science,' but the real battle was now being waged between Gray and Tatlock. Gray's reply to the challenge laid before him came without delay, but only seemed to make the whole thing even more complicated than it already was. He first of all put his reputation on the line.

> I pledge my reputation as a chemist that the analyses submitted by you to me for examination, and published by you in the *Mail*, were substantially correct. Dr Anderson and Mr Tatlock question my competency to conduct such analyses. What I propose is this ...

His proposals, eight in all, involved the concocting and dividing of further sample of whisky in a move which seemed destined to protract the life of something that was already dead. Glasgow's mystery had almost run its course. He must have expected, and perhaps hoped, that his proposals would not be taken up. He had avoided the challenge issued by Tatlock, and finished with an escape clause.

> If this challenge be not accepted I must decline to waste further time on mere wordy controversy,
>
> > Yours very sincerely,
> > James St Clair Gray, M.D.

Why did Gray not accept Tatlock's invite to speak before his chemical society? By now everyone must have been getting a bit fed up with the continuous bickering, and Gray would have been no exception. As far as he was concerned the thing was done and finished with, and nothing useful could be gained by a face to face confrontation with a man who he must now have loathed. He may also have felt a bit uneasy at the prospect of speaking in front of a group of men who would undoubtedly have sided with Tatlock. He had given talks to societies before, but never away from home, so to speak, nor to such an intimidating gathering. Might he also have sensed defeat? Was he having doubts about his own results? We can never know, and personally, I think not. Gray was not finished.

Tatlock's reply was, again, immediate, appearing in the 'Mail on the same day as Gray's proposals. In a short letter, he highlighted Gray's unwillingness to have his report scrutinised by the highest chemical authorities in the country, and also mentioned his evasion of the invite to speak. His final words on the investigation were curt and written as if Gray had already been condemned.

> Should Dr Gray be called upon to analyse whisky again, I have no doubt that he will be more careful, and profit by the experience of the chemists who have taken part in the controversy. The whole question will be submitted to the chemical public by and by, and the result will no doubt find its way into the newspapers. Till then, I decline any further controversy on the subject,
> I am, etc., Robert R. Tatlock.

By this stage the subject of whisky must have been on the lips of every Glasgow citizen, and some thought it all rather amusing. Earlier on in the month of October, Eliza Davies had been brought before the

Central Police Court under a charge of hawking spirits without a licence. She was, to give her her grand title, a peripatetic shebeener. During the legal proceedings, Bailie Salmon took a sniff from the bottle which had been found in her possession, and announced that he was not chemist enough to know what it might consist of. "It might be the same as specimen No. 19," remarked the Chief Constable, which brought a laugh from within the Court.[5]

At the end of October, Glasgow's newspaper *The Bailie* briefly entered into the spirit of things by furnishing one of its employees with coins of the realm and instructions to investigate some of these spirituous mysteries. The gentleman did not wish to harm his constitution and so made a positive attempt to obtain good liquor, which he duly sampled, courtesy of his palate. Served in the form of a hot, steaming toddy, the drink was said to be 'gran' whusky,' and was swiftly followed by a second, and a third. A Welsh rabbit was then consumed before another tumbler of warm mountain-dew was suitably tested. The unfortunate man then tumbled out into the street, sang songs, drank some stout, and took part in a general night of debauchery which ended in the cells of a police station.[6] On a more serious note, *The Bailie's* next edition offered a solution to end the great whisky debate.

> It is simply that a fresh collection of shebeen and other whisky samples should be procured, and that the three combatants (Doctor Gray, Professor Anderson, and Mr Tatlock), and the editor of the *Herald* too, if he cares to join them, should set to work, the victory falling to the first man who is under the table. The BAILIE sincerely hopes, in the interests of newspaper readers, that this suggestion may be taken, and that thereafter no more may be heard of a dispute which has become a nuisance.[7]

The *Glasgow Herald* had been severely critical of Doctor Gray in a lengthy article which was published immediately prior to *The Bailie's* comments. In it they attempted to take an overall view of the whole whisky story, their siding with Anderson and Tatlock being evident by their bias in omitting any mention of the many letters of support for Gray. They regarded his latest proposal as 'the most amusing contribution' that had appeared during the controversy, and saw him as impudent in supporting he could pit himself against Professor

Anderson. They drew all sorts of comparisons between the two men, one being their difference in stature which was said to be akin to that between David and Goliath. The *Glasgow Herald* was hitting a man who was down; or so they thought.

Doctor James St. Clair Gray's final words were printed in the *'Mail* on November 1st 1872, just over five weeks after the first report. On reading his letter you can almost feel the seething anger and frustration which he must have felt at the hopelessness of his predicament. Glasgow's whisky *had* contained the stated adulterants, but there was now no way that he could actually prove it, and in the eyes of certain members of the public it was *he* who was at fault, and not Glasgow's whisky. How had he ever got himself into such a mess? The *Glasgow Herald's* article was pulled apart.

> The distortion of facts in the *Herald's* leading article of to-day is so glaring that had its readers had any opportunity of acquainting themselves with the real merits of the case I should not have considered it necessary to make any explanation. As, however, you have published neither my analyses nor reports, neither Professor Anderson's attacks on them nor my replies – nor, in a word, anything that has been written in my defence except my reply to Dr Tatlock's report, it becomes necessary that I should do so.

Glasgow's broadsheet was then put well in its place, Doctor Gray dealing quite satisfactorily with all the points raised, his dignity and esteem remaining intact. He drew attention to their unfortunate use of the David and Goliath analogy, and reminded them that the giant involved in this biblical confrontation came off second best. Gray bowed out, unbroken.

Glasgow's mystery was over, except for one thing ... the proof.

7

Forbes Mackenzie and the Backlands of Glasgow

CENTRAL Glasgow in the mid-Victorian period was overcrowded. Too many people were packed into the closes and wynds that led off the streets in the area of The Cross. On the surface everything looked fairly respectable with a great variety of shops lining each of the thoroughfares. In the Trongate, the first street in the city to have a proper pavement for the privilege of the wealthy, there were banks, music sellers, whip makers, hosiers, drapers, wig makers, tobacconists, druggists, spirit merchants, corkcutters, hatters, a waxworks, and a whole host of different trades. In the somewhat less-opulent Saltmarket, High Street, and Gallowgate, there were also many businesses, although perhaps of a more basic nature, like bootmakers, bakers, undertakers, pawnbrokers, victuallers, and a rather large number of spirit dealers.

However, behind this façade of normality lay a veritable warren of poverty. Every available space was built on. Living conditions were little better than they had been in medieval times, residents often lacking simple essentials like a sink and having to cart their slops down to street-level where they would blend with all the other abounding filth. The only space *not* built on was occupied by the dung-hill which rose up in its clearing amidst the surrounding tenements like some stupendous, festering boil on the face of humanity, occasionally bursting and setting forth a stinking river of pollution into the cellars at its edge. Here, people tried to live.

A study, done in 1846, reveals the true horrors faced by residents. In Sugarhouse Close, off the Gallowgate, a two-apartment house comprising a kitchen and bedroom was found to have a mud floor which smelled more of a churchyard than of a place of habitation. The bedroom had one window which was almost completely obscured by

130

adjoining buildings, neither light nor air finding a clear path through its opening. For this dark pit of a hovel, £3 6s a year rent was charged.[1]

Pensioner Darby Thomas and his wife lived in Gordon's Close, Saltmarket, in a room measuring 9 by 14 feet. The donkey which he once used in his coal retailing business also stayed in this room before the poor beast died. The couple's bed consisted of a few planks covered with straw, and a few pieces of dirty sacking, the whole thing lying on top of a wet mud floor.[2] Is it any wonder that many sought solace in the bright and magnificent surroundings of a public house where they could live a short fantasy of pretended riches?

> One can scarcely realise the enormous number of these houses, with their flaring gas lights in frosted globes, and brightly gilded spirit casks, lettered by the number of gallons, under the cognomen of 'Old Tom' or 'Young Tom', as the case may be, with the occasional mirror at the extreme end of the shop, reflecting at once in fine perspective the waters of a granite fountain fronting the door, and the entrance of poor broken-down victims, who stand in pitiful burlesque in their dirty rags, amid all this pomp and mocking grandeur![3]

The publican was just as eager to serve the poor as he was the rich, and knew than an essential part of his business came from the former quarter. It was therefore in his interests to make his establishment as welcoming as possible and as unlike the surroundings to which some of his clientele would unfortunately have to return at the end of the night, and in this respect his own appearance was no exception. In Shadow's 1858 delve into Glasgow's seedier side, one rather stout and well-fed landlord is seen to be dressed in a white shirt with a highly coloured 'Valentia waistcoat.' His fingers bear a profusion of rings, and he welcomes each and every customer, no matter how 'emaciated, ragged or destitute', with a 'welcome cheerful twinkle in his eye.' The publican was no fool.

In this same public house, whose entrance is marred by a huddle of children who patiently wait for their mother, and whose interior is dogged by semiconscious inebriates, a steady trickle of women stagger from the street towards the counter for something to take back to their den. One presents a broken teacup into which the landlord places 4d worth of whisky. Another hands over an enormous pitcher and leaves with a half-pint, or 'three-halfpence' worth, of ale. A minute or so later another two appear and depart with whisky, one measure in a pickle-bottle, the other in some unidentifiable glass container. Whisky was not then the respectable spirit that we know today, and was consumed, on the whole, by the poorer working classes.[4] Around seven million gallons were drunk in Scotland each year, an amount equivalent to about twenty pints for every man, woman and child.

Such was the craving for drink and the need for relief from reality, that many people were prepared to pawn the shirt off their back. In Pipehouse Close, at 93 High Street, 150 familes were housed, the total number of residents being around 750. A pawnbroker was also located in the close, and beside this was a strategically-placed spirit dealer. Emaciated wretches would trade-in what clothes they had, leaving the barest minimum, and spend their meagre 'windfall' next door.[5]

The sight of such activity when it spilled out into the street was most unwelcome to more-fortunate citizens who disliked this visual reminder of how life really was for a long-neglected and sizeable segment of society. They wanted none of it, especially on the Sabbath when they would parade their finery around the city and look down on the dregs at their feet. In May 1849 the *Scottish Temperance Review* reported that on one particular Sunday 'no fewer than 280 persons were observed to enter a single house in Glasgow in the course of an hour and half' to obtain spirituous liquor.[6]

The link between crime and intemperance was regarded as one of a number of good reasons for changing the law with regard to the retail of alcoholic beverages. Glasgow's backlands concealed innumerable illicit drinking dens and any number of brothels, most also selling wines and spirits without a licence. There were other problems associated with drink. With such poor standards of living and a less-than-substantial diet, alcohol sent many to an early grave. In 1849 Charles Ritchie, a one-time physician at Glasgow's Royal Infirmary, said that about fifty per cent of cases received at the hospital were connected more or less directly with the use of spirituous liquor. Alcohol did, of course, have its advocates in the medical profession. One Doctor Buchanan, Professor of Anatomy in the Andersonian University, used to give 12 oz of wine and 7 oz whisky daily to severe cases in the surgical wards.[7]

Glasgow was not alone in facing difficulties of an intemperate nature, and in 1853 the Government introduced measures to combat

Glasgow's Saltmarket in 1868. (Annan Collection, Mitchell Library).

drunkenness, and its resultant evils, at the very heart of its existence
.... the public house.

The Failure of Forbes Mackenzie

The 1853 Forbes Mackenzie Act was designed for the regulation of
public houses and other businesses, like grocers and hotels, who were
involved in the retailing of liquor in Scotland. The licence certificate
for publicans contained many conditions, one of the most important
being that their hours of opening were to be restricted to between 8
a.m. and 11 p.m. from Monday to Saturday, and on Sundays they were
to stay closed all day. It looked like a major breakthrough, and in many
respects it was, but behind the statistics and tables and reports of peace
on the Sabbath lay an unforeseen knock-on effect.

Many publicans went out of business after 1853 due to a fall in
earnings brought about by the reduced opening hours, and also
because they were refused licences on the grounds that their premises
had been found to be unsuitable. While the number of licenced
hostelries fell, there was a corresponding increase in the number of
unlicenced shebeens, as seen in the following table relating to
Glasgow.[8]

	Licences Granted	Unlicensed Convictions	Estimated Shebeens
1852	1,930	24	48
1853	1,994	25	50
1854	1,995	57	114
1855	1,887	121	242
1856	1,773	112	224
1857	1,673	223	446

The estimated figure for the number of shebeens, a simple doubling of
those actually caught, was probably far short of the truth. An official
return of 1858 gave the names and addresses of 326 people who had
been 'positively ascertained by the police to be habit and repute in the
undisguised practice of illicit spirit-selling.' The actual figure was
thought to be double or treble that number.[9]

Glasgow's population was increasing at the rate of around 10,000
per annum, and by cutting the number of legal places to drink by about
100 each year the authorities were practically forcing people to use
shebeens; not everyone wanted to spend a 'relaxing' evening in a

seething mass of bodies all battling to reach the overcrowded counter. In addition, the new hours were not to everyone's liking. Those who worked throughout the night, and on Sundays, now found they couldn't get a drink at their usual time and had no option but to make alternative arrangements for that much-needed refreshment. Members of the Press came into this category, but made their complaint to no avail.

It didn't take long for the public to find ways around the legislation, some legal, some not. In Wigton, a few licenced publicans kept cows, and it was brought to the attention of the authorities that there was an unusual increase in the number of people buying 'milk' on Sundays. Many publicans all over the country took a gamble and opened up - behind closed doors - on Sundays and after 11 p.m. during the week. In 1872 the size of fine they might have expected if caught, was of the order of £2, a figure which no doubt paled into insignificance when compared with the counter-takings collected after 11 p.m. on a Saturday night. There's nothing busier than a pub at closing time.

The years following 1853 saw an upsurge in the number of working-men's clubs where drink could be had at almost any hour, including Sundays. Some may have been set up with the sole intention of evading the law with respect to the new Act, and were referred to as 'palpable shams' where anyone could join by paying a nominal fee.

It was therefore to the club, or shebeen, or even the druggist, that most citizens turned when they wanted a drink outwith public house hours. Grocers were allowed to sell alcohol from 6 a.m. during the week, but there can't have been many people up and about at that time to benefit from the extra few hours. On Sundays, some people took to travelling to nearby villages where, as 'travellers', they were allowed to partake of a tipple in an inn or hotel. Reducing the number of licenced houses, and their hours, was not an answer to society's insobriety, as all it did was move the tipplers to a different location to sup their poison. If man wants to drink alcohol, he will, and no amount of legislation will affect this in any way.

Having said that, the new Act was hailed a success. In 1855 Glasgow's Superintendent of Police, James Smart, stated that since coming into the force, cases of drunkenness on the streets on Sundays were very rare. Rev. David McRae, of the Gorbals, was of a similar opinion and saw a marked change in his local Main Street where previously citizens were frequently being 'jostled against by drunk persons, giving utterance to the language of profane swearing and the coarsest vulgarity.'[10]

Others thought the Act had failed miserably, and there was some talk about the juggling of figures to give the impression that drunkenness was reduced. Different systems were said to be used by different burghs for recording the number of drunks, and even within one burgh there could be a lack of uniformity. It was therefore very difficult to tell with any certainty whether the number of cases was falling or rising, although on the surface the former *seemed* to be the case. In Dunfermline, for example, figures were altered so as to occupy four columns as opposed to one, and while at first glance it might seem that there was a reduction, there was in fact an increase of twenty-two per cent.[11] In James Stirling's 1859 publication titled *Failure of the Forbes Mackenzie Act*, he examines such 'grotesque incongruities' and speculates that figures for 'drunk and disorderly' will eventually 'disappear mysteriously from the police sheet' so as to show the Act's success. In 1868 in Glasgow, they did.[12]

The Police at Midnight

The combined application of the Forbes Mackenzie Act with a doubling in the price of whisky from 3d to 6d per gill in 1854 and 1855 sent many drinkers scurrying to their nearest shebeen.[13] In such uncontrolled surroundings the liquor was often grossly adulterated, but cheap, and you could drink till the cows came home. By increasing the duty on whisky immediately following the 1853 Act, the Government was perhaps attempting to tackle inebriety on a number of fronts by putting it out of reach of some less-affluent drinkers, while maintaining a comparable level of revenue. Adulteration was probably not even considered, although it was well-known that large increases in duty invariably provided a greater incentive to the criminal fraternity. In trying to solve one problem, the Government was creating another.

By 1860 the number of people caught selling spirits without a licence in Glasgow was reduced to one, and although the police must have been putting a lot of effort into their detection, it is hard to believe that the figure was so low. James Smart echoed this notion by saying in the same year that serious assaults were on the increase: and 'will still further increase till some means are devised to put down the sale of spirits in unlicenced premises.' The police had few powers where shebeens were concerned, and had to rely heavily on the use of informers. They might bribe a child to enter a suspected house with a tale of needing some brandy for a dying mother; or two scoundrels could be paid to drink in a shebeen, the owner being convicted solely on their evidence.[14] The police were not loved for such disingenuous tactics, and battles occasionally took place between the two parties, often culminating in the cracking of a few skulls, on both sides of the fence.

In 1861 the number of convictions in this area was only six, but a serious problem still lurked beneath the surface. One murder had occurred near the door of an unlicenced whisky shop, and the perpetrator of a stabbing was found to have been drinking in a shebeen before carrying out the offence. As one detective in Edinburgh later put it, 'The assumption is that we are becoming too sharp for the shebeeners; the fact is that they have become too sharp for us.' There were lots of them out there, the police simply weren't catching them.

A measure of just how misleading such low figures can be may be seen in the years following 1862, when an Act was passed which made amendments to the previous 1853 public house statute, and also gave the police greater powers to tackle shebeens. They could now enter suspected premises to look for, and seize, the tools of the trade, like drinking utensils and 'fittings usually found in houses licenced for the sale of exciseable liquors,' and could arrest anyone found drunk or drinking on the premises. If more than one gallon of liquor was found, this too was seized.

Between 1862 and 1871, as a direct result of vigorous assiduity of the new Act, the number of shebeen convictions in Glasgow rose considerably and began to give a clearer picture of just how many were in business. Once again, the *actual* figure was almost certainly far greater.[15]

	Selling Spirits without a Licence	Found Drinking in a Shebeen
1862	192	6
1863	179	93
1864	203	37
1865	281	6
1866	200	9
1867	131	92
1868	133	323
1869	169	310
1870	–	–
1871	250	489

Laigh Kirk Close, 59 Trongate, Glasgow, in 1868. The densely overcrowded and squalid properties around this alley concealed numerous brothels and shebeens. It was here that Inspector Steel was injured while on shebeen duty in 1871. (*Annan Collection, Mitchell Library*).

The figures seem to jump about a bit, but the trend, certainly in the right-hand column, is an increase. After 1871 there is a noticeable reduction which may be credited to the police. Their efforts were obviously paying off.

In the early hours of a Sunday morning, small groups of police officers could be found furtively creeping around the closes and alleys in central Glasgow carrying out their shebeen duty. It was not an easy task. Lookouts were usually posted near the close-mouth entrance to give warning of police presence, and by the time they had gained entry all signs of a spirituous business were well out of sight. Such raids were at times violent affairs, and it wasn't always the offenders who struck the first blow. Back in the 1850s a police lieutenant had been a touch over-zealous in carrying out his duty and had waded in amongst a group of so-called villains with cries of "Walk into the Sepoys" and other rallying shouts. After bouncing his 'skull-cracker' off a few heads, it emerged that one rather innocent citizen had been caught up in the affray and had been grievously injured. The officer was charged. On another occasion, this time in July 1871, an Inspector Steel had been hit about the head with a poker while doing his rounds, with Sergeant Cameron, in the backlands of Laigh Kirk Close. Thankfully, serious injury was rare.

Accounts of raids, especially those of some note, often found their way into newspapers, and with 1871 being such a busy year there was certainly a number of interesting reports. On 12th June 1871, the following appeared in the *North British Daily Mail*.

ANOTHER SHEBEEN RAID

About midnight on Saturday Lieuts. Donald and Macdonald and Inspectors Steele and MacDougall made a tour of inspection through the lower parts of the city, for the purpose of taking into custody the breakers of the law by shebeening. In Trongate the shebeen of Wm. John Craig was found with a crowd of thirsty customers about the door, and on closer inspection a woman was found dispensing the precious liquid from a bottle. The shop was in darkness, but on lighting the gas some jars of whisky were discovered and half-a-dozen people who had evidently been partaking of their contents. The woman managing the house and her customers were taken into custody. Craig and his wife and a number of other parties are at present 'doing time' in prison for managing this shebeen. The house of Margaret McKendrick, in New

Wynd, was next visited, and several parties were found, and also jars of whisky and other drinks. In this place there was found on the counter a glass bottle, which attracted attention from its peculiar appearance. It was found, on investigation, that it had contained medicine for a fever patient, and some whisky by mistake having been put into it, the mixture was thought too valuable to be thrown away, and had been used to supply the less discriminating class of customers.

In some shebeens, as we have already seen, clients were lucky if they got *any* whisky in their 'whisky', so perhaps this medicinal concoction was luxury to a few.

At times those who kept a shebeen were particularly adept at evading the clutches of the law. It wasn't as if the police weren't aware of their existence; they were, but every time they entered the premises they were unable to discover any exciseable liquor. In June 1871 one such case came to light in Glasgow's Central District. During a raid on Ann Armstrong's house in Jeffrey's Close, Bridgegate, a notorious shebeen which had been operational for many years, it emerged that Ann in fact occupied both the ground floor and the house directly above. Customers entered at ground level and were served drink from the upper apartment through a hole in the floor, hence why nothing had ever been found.[16] Another similar ruse was used in the Trongate where the perpetrator also occupied two flats, one above the other. On this occasion a hoist, capable of holding a gross of bottles, ran between the jaw-boxes (sinks) of both flats. Whenever the police carried out a raid, the hoist was raised or lowered to the other flat, much to the presumed irritation of the officers in attendance who could find no evidence whatsoever. This continued for many years, and was only brought to an abrupt end when the building was demolished during the city's improvement scheme.[17]

Shebeeners were certainly a crafty lot, and there are many tales involving some of the strangest methods of concealment where characters displayed phenomenal fighting-spirit in a world that had essentially failed them. There was Maggie, who carried out her business in the Saltmarket. She lived in a top flat, and unfortunately had her gas cut off through falling behind with payments. With the inventive brain-power of a university professor, and a desire to make the best of a bad thing, she then had a small tin cistern made, capable of holding about four gallons, and placed it in the roof-space above her room. A piece of piping was then connected between this and the disused gas-pipe which terminated over the mantelpiece. Once the cistern was filled, whisky was forthcoming simply by turning on the 'gas'. She would probably never have been caught had an acquaintance not informed on her.[18]

One woman kept her poison in a teapot by the fire; if police officers were to suddenly make an appearance, then this simmering symbol of domesticity would hardly merit a second glance. Another young maiden used to wander around the Saltmarket area supposedly selling milk, which was in fact whisky at 6d a glass. Shebeeners of a peripatetic nature were a problem of some concern as they usually prayed on unsuspecting citizens who already had a bit too much to drink. They were termed 'ghouls of the night.' When the victim had been enticed up some dark close with promises of 'guid whusky', they were then dosed with a vile mixture of sulphuric acid and methylated spirits. Once reduced to a collapsed state, they would be relieved of any valuables, and often their shoes and coat were removed.

Then there were characters like Blind Mike. He was sightless, although whether this affliction was due to some natural malady or a liking for his own blend of hooch is not clear. All his customers were known by voice, and his method of pouring them a measure of 'whisky' was, to say the least, unique .... 'He keeps the glass to his mouth, lifts the whisky bottle, pours the liquour into the glass, and when it has reached the rim he knows by it touching his lips.'[19] Mike was hailed as a bit of a prince among shebeeners, and was well-known all over the city. Anyone unfamiliar entering the house would find themselves subjected to a thorough inspection, as Mike's fingers probed their outer garments for policeman's buttons.

A Visit to the Fountain

Scattered throughout the literature of mid-Victorian Scotland is a small number of interesting accounts of visits to shebeens. Each one gives a fascinating insight into what is usually the most basic type of drinking-house of the period, and although there existed those whose interior décor equalled, and at times far exceeded, that found within some of the better public houses, the bulk of them were indeed of a rudimentary, and sometimes abominable, quality.

Alexander Brown, under his literary disguise of 'Shadow', describes one such visit in his 1858 work titled *Midnight Scenes and Social Photographs*. In his eagerness to bring to light the appalling conditions in which many of Glasgow's poor were forced to eke out a living, and to highlight the twilight world of alcohol abuse which both caused and relieved such misery, Alexander set foot in some of the worst shebeens imaginable. Sadly, the following pathetic scene is more than likely typical of how life was for a substantial proportion of the populace in the 1850s.

> Not much above two hundred yards from the Central Station, and just as the clock strikes the melancholy hour of one, we visit, in company with an official, A LOW SHEBEEN. It is situated in a dark close, resembling a subterranean passage to some untraversed cavern. As we enter, our footsteps are heard, and, anticipating our errand, a ruffianly-looking fellow emerges from a cellar, locks the door, fumbles about, and pretends to be giving security to the shutters. Unfortunately for him, as we approach, a light is observed to escape from above and below the door. "Halloa!" says our guide, "what is this? open." The door is forthwith opened, and to our astonishment there stands before us on a damp earthen floor nearly half-a-dozen women, most of them in middle life, and one or two comparatively aged. They are trying to appear calm and collected amid the excitement of obvious terror. They are poorly clad, pale, hungry looking, and emaciated. The place is lit by a candle stuck against the wall, giving it a desolate appearance. A new deal counter divides the apartment. At one end, near the door, a high temporary partition is raised, to form a sort of 'snug' inside, where seats are placed for three or four persons before a small fire. We glance about for 'the bottle', or for vestiges of any kind by which the shebeen-keeper plies his nefarious calling, but to no purpose. At the extreme end of the counter we discover a wine glass, but nothing more.

In 1869 the *North British Daily Mail* published two lengthy articles on shebeening in Glasgow. The writer, calling himself 'A Minion of the Moon', gave detailed descriptions of premises he had visited during many years as a regular, and even provided the reader with an introductory lecture on the laws of the land in relation to this illicit trade. He gave a rough estimate of between 300 and 350 for the number of shebeens in the city, most lying within the Central District in closes, wynds and alleys leading from the Trongate, Saltmarket, King Street, Bridgegate, and other thoroughfares. He offered a derivation for the word 'shebeen', which apparently came from an Irish term for a humble whisky cabin, and went on to divide them into two main categories - 'the shebeen pure and simple, and that wherein the traffic is carried on along with or under cover of some legitimate business.' Examples were given of both.

Sunday morning, say from six till nine o'clock, is perhaps about as busy a time as any with the shebeen-keeper proper of the lower class. Of this I had a sample two Sundays ago. I was out betimes that morning, and accidentally meeting an acquaintance at the Cross, soon after six o'clock we strolled down Saltmarket towards the river. At the foot of the street we halted to consider whether or not we should do a walk round the Green, when there passed us two men, who might from their appearance be journeymen carpenters, and who evidently had not been in bed for some time. "These fellows look dry," I said. "Yes," my friend returned, "but they're not far from the fountain now – watch them." I did so and observed them turn up a lane hard by. I proposed that we should follow them to the fountain, and it was agreed to. A few doors up the lane on the left hand there is a "close," at the foot of which stood a fat red-faced woman, who irresistibly suggested Moll Flagon to my mind. She was peering now up the lane and now down, and I knew at once that this was the guardian angel of the fountain. Whenever she saw that we made for going up the close, she said hurriedly, "Now look sharp, chaps; there's a new sergeant on this mornin'." We instantly assumed a sharp appearance, and proceeded up three pair of stairs, then through a dark lobby into a small kitchen, where we found the fountain in full play. There would be from a dozen to fifteen drouthy topers inside to whose wants two men were busily administering. The question they put to each customer was simply "beer or whisky?" If the former you had it out of the can, 2d per glass; of the latter, out of the bottle, 3d per glass, hand over your money and be off at once to make room for fresh comers. There was no such thing as sitting down thought of and no accommodation for such a thing. It was simply "a drain" and begone. We met those who had had it as we came up stairs, and we met those in quest of it as we were going down, and there at the close mouth was Moll Flagon imploring later pilgrims as she had implored us to "look sharp, for that there was a new sergeant on that morning." Considering that the liquor sold out of the bottle more resembled grog than whisky, while that out of the can would have met Christopher Sly's demand for "a pot of the smallest ale," I think that large profits and quick returns would best characterise the business done at the fountain.

143

Leaving Moll Flagon on the look out, we resolved to postpone the proposed walk round the Green *sine die*, and turned northwards again. On reaching the Cross we fell in with a friend of my companion, who, for my benefit, explained that living not far off, it was his custom always of a Sunday morning in good weather to take a stroll down here and leisurely observe the peculiar aspects of the scene. We told him where we had been, which quite naturally brought up the subject of shebeening generally, and an offer from my new friend, "while our hand was in at any rate," to show us another place where a good stroke was usually done between midnight on Saturday and breakfast time on Sunday morning. Accordingly, we walked up High Street a certain distance, and then turned up a long dirty close on the left-hand side of the street. A short distance up the close widened and became open overhead, and near the top it was much like an oblong court-yard. On the left hand side of this was a little shop below the level of the court-yard, so that you went down a step to enter it. On entering you could scarcely say whether the place was a shop or a shed – a hovel, with a little worm-eaten dirty counter separating the window from the door would perhaps be a better designation for it than either. On the theory that it was a shop, the only commodities I could see on sale were a few pickled herrings in a basin, a handful of green onions, a small bunch of halfpenny candles, and some potatoes in a corner. As we were going in two "navvies" were coming out, one of them wiping his mouth with the sleeve of his jacket, which was an intelligible symptom. Satisfied apparently that we were "right", the mistress of the place found a chair and a couple of stools for us to sit down upon. She then said, "Weel, what is't?" "O," said our cicerone, in reply, "*hard*, I suppose." The woman held out her hand – "a shilling" – and the coin was given her. She then went to the door and beckoned to a man who was quietly smoking his pipe at a door opposite, and whom she hailed by the name of Michael, to come over. Michael seemed perfectly to understand the situation, for without anything further passing between the two he came and smoked his pipe at our door and the woman came inside. She immediately went to a recess in the wall at the very back of the shop or shed, where darkness was semi-visible, and produced a quart bottle and glass, as also a tumbler and jug of water. She had filled out for them, and my companions had drank a glass each, and the bottle was raised to pour out my modicum of the nectar, when Michael at the door turned round and gave a cough. In a moment the bottle and glass and tumbler were back in the recess, and we three commenced to smoke our pipes and to look as nearly as we could pictures of innocence. In less than five minutes thereafter Michael turned round and coughed again, when the woman's anxious expression of countenance cleared away at once, she forthwith reproduced the bottle, and the ceremony which had been so abruptly broken off was completed. In recognition of Michael's services it was agreed that he should have a glass, and the proposal was supplemented by my friend number two, who declared that we would join with our faithful watchman, the "round" being at his (number two's) charges. To this there was no dissentient voice, and a "nei'bour lassie" having being found to relieve guard for a little, Michael was called in and the bottle again brought forth. To the general disappointment, however, it was found to contain barely a glass and a half in all, and the jar from which it had been replenished was absolutely empty – the hostess was sold out, a state of matters which went to confirm number two's averment that the place was wont to do a "good stroke" o' Sundays. With an amount of liberality and "live and let live" feeling which surely redounded to her credit, the woman would not see us beaten although we had to go past her own door, and directed us to a kindred establishment on the opposite side of the same court, where we had *deoch an doras* and Michael the guerdon of his good services. His first signal he informed us was caused by the entrance of a policeman from High Street into the close. The "bobby," however, did not come up our length, but ascended the staircase leading to the houses facing the street, and on coming down again returned as he came into High Street. Then came the second signal, intimating that the coast was clear. Such is a fair sample of how the thing is done in the lower class shebeens, the general similarity of which in their surroundings and *modus operandi* rendering it unnecessary that I should at present encroach upon any more space in describing them.[20]

The writer then went on to describe a comical scene which developed in a third-rate shebeen in Glasgow's eastern quarter, when one impoverished individual traded-in his trousers for one more wee refreshment. Unfortunately, while supping his drink and planning how he might acquire a replacement garment, a shout went up that the house was to be swiftly cleared – possibly because of an impending raid – and the man had to make good his escape with a kilt-like newspaper pinned to his rear.

Alcohol was illicitly sold as a side-line in a number of legitimate businesses who lacked the necessary paperwork to make the activity legal. A coffee-house in Glasgow's city centre was known to serve a good fish supper. Once the food had been eaten, a discreet nod to an attendant would bring a bottle of beer or a glass of whisky to your table, the drink being consumed immediately so as not to leave any tell-tale empties lying around. There must have been a number of such shops, and although coming loosely under the heading of a shebeen, they at least carried out their criminal activity in fairly decorous surroundings.

At one point the number of shebeens in the north-eastern district was seen to fall, as highlighted in the second article by the same writer, dating to 29th June 1869. Police activity had initiated the decline, although all was not as it appeared to be. Apparently a policeman from 'F' Division had told an old shebeener that he could get a licence to sell table-beer from the Excise for only 2s 6d. With this piece of paper under his belt, the law could not bring shebeening charges, even if the liquor was stronger than that allowed by the licence. The old man promptly obtained the necessary certificate and found that the advice was good, so much so that he passed on the information to his business buddies. Before long, the demand for table-beer licences soared, and the Excise, taking advantage of this sudden and, as far as they were concerned, rather peculiar increase, doubled the cost to 5s. On the surface it seemed as if there were fewer illicit liquor houses, but of course the licence was simply used as a cloak for common shebeening, as aptly demonstrated by the fact that one 'land' had twelve houses, all supposedly selling table-beer. And while on this subject, it may be of interest to add that table-beer was no different to other beverages when it came to adulteration. Often a smaller beer was employed as a diluent, body being restored by the addition of coarse brown sugar and black soap.[21]

In another establishment visited by 'A Minion of the Moon', he finds himself in an 'old-fashioned back place not far from the Cross,' where he joins a companion in a bid to wash down a couple of 'finnan haddies' with a little illicit spirit. It was their first time at this particular howff, and the woman of the house initially repudiated any idea of such practices in her place. She eventually consented to see what could be done, and placed the drouthy duo in a little room under a low roof.

"Just gie twa 'chaps' up there with your stick – canny noo," said the woman, pointing to a corner of the ceiling.

After two suitably canny knocks, a small trap-door, measuring about eight inches by four, opened, and an eye appeared. Once the order had been made, the eye disappeared, and was followed a few seconds later by a tin-can containing a handkerchief, which was lowered down on a string. A shilling was wrapped in the material and placed in the can,

146

which slowly rose back to whence it came. Half an anxious minute later, a cough alerted the occupants of the room, who looked up to see half a mutchin of whisky appear from the heavens.

Also on the subject of liquor concealment, a shebeen in the Central District was allowed to trade for many years under the enterprising efforts of one Nancy McFadyen. As was often the case, the police were aware of the house, but could never find any spirits. During business hours Nancy wore a stout and capacious crinoline, within which, hanging from the top hoop of the support, were two or three pint bottles of whisky carefully arranged so as not to clink when she moved. During the many raids, she took herself, and her stock, into a neighbour's house to let the police exhaust themselves in yet another fruitless search, and would return when it had all blown over. Nancy went on to haunt closes around the Trongate, London Street, Saltmarket, and the like, as a peripatetic shebeener.[22]

There's nae Whusky in't!

Of course it wasn't all fun and games, and shebeens were much more than just interesting houses where spirits were dispensed in all manner of devious ways. In some, the term 'whisky' was simply a cover for any liquid mixture that was vaguely alcoholic. One old hand in Glasgow mentioned to a policeman who had previously been instrumental in getting him convicted, that it was a wrong conviction. He had been charged with selling whisky without a licence, but there had not been a drop of whisky in it – 'it was just spirits of wine with plenty of water.'

But let's not get away from the fact that people were being poisoned. It was in places like those previously described that methylated spirits-based 'finish' was sold under the guise of mountain-dew. Our roving reporter of 1869 had the misfortune to sample some, and it was an experience that he would never forget ....

> Most persons must have heard stories of the frightful character, that is, quality, of shebeen whisky, and in many cases it would be impossible to give it too bad a name. It is the fact that a concoction of the commonest description of raw-grain whisky, methylated spirit and water, known as "finish," is sold as whisky in the lower-class shebeens to men already too drunk to distinguish at the moment what it is they are pouring down their throats. They know next day, however, to their cost. Twice only, in my experience, have I had a glass of this vile mixture, and on both

147

occasions I thought I had been poisoned. The simple smell of "finish" once perceived is never forgotten; and another test is to mingle it was water – the mixture presenting a pale blue appearance well known to the initiated. To obviate this, the shebeen keeper sometimes puts to his "whisky" a little of the cheapest sherry, or burnt sugar.[23]

In 1872 when the *North British Daily Mail* carried out its whisky investigation, it was well-known that some shebeen spirits were deliberately contaminated with methylated spirits or so-called 'finish', but it was only hearsay, and no one had ever categorically stated or proved that this was indeed the case. And why should they? Such dens of iniquity traded outwith legal circles, and if official moves were made to examine such practices then the fact that the shebeen was an illegal business would be a major stumbling block. You cannot examine the liquor in a house which, according to licensing lists, does not exist. So the authorities got on with the business of charging shebeeners and their customers, and pretty well ignored exactly what was being drunk. If it looked and smelled like whisky, then that was good enough, and a charge was brought for selling or drinking whisky in a shebeen.

But when similar methylic malpractices were suspected of becoming all too prevalent in public houses – places already notorious for adulteration in one form or another – then clearly something had to be done. Unfortunately it wasn't those in power who made the first move, and the problem was grasped very firmly by a newspaper editor who saw the potential for putting right yet another of the world's wrongs, and for possibly creating his biggest scoop yet.

And so it was that the *North British Daily Mail* set about putting onto paper, in black and white, the true condition of whisky in Glasgow. Men involved with retail and regulation within the spirit trade, who had chose to ignore for far too long the deteriorating situation that was developing on their doorstep, were now forced to sit up and take notice, and many didn't like it one bit. Even with analytical confirmation, they still weren't prepared to believe it, and one or two took great pleasure in belittling the young analyst who had carried out the tests.

However, almost two weeks after Doctor Gray's final letter, an ally appeared from a most unexpected quarter. It was a shebeen keeper who himself decided to spill the beans and give the world an insight into what whisky was *really* like, when served in the backlands of Glasgow.

8

The Damning Evidence

THE following letter appeared in the *North British Daily Mail* on the 13th November 1872. It was also reproduced in a later pamphlet titled *Doings of a Notorious Glasgow Shebeener*, a copy of which was acquired by Glasgow's Mitchell Library in 1892, but it is very much part of our whisky mystery, and was written in response to the arguments that raged during the latter stages of the investigation. I make no apologies for quoting it in full. Its content is of insurmountable importance.

A SHEBEENER'S REMINISCENCES

Sir, – There has been a good deal about shebeen whisky in your paper lately, and as I ought to know something about it I don't mind giving you a few of my experiences, seeing that I have now retired from the business and don't mean going back to it. My first acquaintance with doctored drink was at a shebeen in my native Saltmarket, kept by a man of the name of Johnnie Crichton. That was in the year 1850 – twenty-two years ago. The place was a dancing crib, and when the dancers got warm they used to cool themselves with a mixture of Johnny's own invention; and I'll tell you how he made it. Into five gallons of water he put one gallon of raw grain whisky and 6d worth of methylated spirits of wine and about a pint or so of raspberry vinegar to colour. This he called "half-and-half," and he sold it at 6d the gill. At that time you could get a gallon of raw grain whisky for 6s 6d, and the vinegar and methylated would hardly cost 1s 6d more, so that Johnny sold his mixture at a nice profit, as you may calculate. Three of four years after this, in the year 1854, I was door-keeper at a drum in King Street which had a short life and a merry one, and through the day I had the making up of the whisky. This was my receipt for the article. To two gallons of whisky, which then cost us 10s 6d a gallon, I added three gallons of water and 6d worth of methylated. This gave us five gallons of stuff, which cost us 21s 6d only. We sold it at 8d the gill, and as 32 gills go to the gallon, we made it pay too, though not as sweet as Johnnie's. It was soon after this that the drinking clubs started, owing to Forbes McKenzie shutting up the licensed shops at 11 o'clock. In 1855 I was connected with a rattler in the Saltmarket, on the left hand side going down. It was a licensed house when I went to it as barman, but three months afterwards it lost the licence, and we then started it as the "Independent Club," with me as the acting manager. We were open night and day, Saturday and Sunday – never shut at all. We had 13 waiters and relieved each other in night and day shifts. I went on duty at 11 o'clock at night and left off at 7 in the morning, except on Saturdays and Sundays. On Saturdays I went in at 2 p.m. and never left the place till about 3 o'clock on Monday morning. From 11 o'clock on Saturday night till 2 o'clock on Sunday morning, our drawings averaged £5 per hour, and our weekly drawings would average about £80. The entry money was one shilling, and as that came to me I was in clover. I was making one way and the other then between £12 and £13 per week. There was mighty little fuss about becoming an "Independent." If a stranger dropped in we would ask if he saw anybody who knew him in the house, and whether they knew him or not if he could get a proposer and seconder we made him a member on the spot. I gave him a ticket with his name written on it, and he have me the shilling – a fair exchange that suited me well. It was all fish that came into the net. We kept all sorts of liquors here, including champagne and sparkling hock. The chief customers for the "fiz" were the swell English thieves. With so much money flying about I was generally able to give them change for a big note, and they would generally have a bottle over it. We had two kinds of whisky here. The best of it was much the same as that I used to make in King Street, but the second class was the real kill-me-deady for choking off the Briggate boys when we would rather have their room than their company. This business was too good to last, and so we were turned out of the place by the landlord. I was connected with other two clubs after this – first the "Waverley," and then the "Old Scotch Grey" Clubs. But neither of them was up to the mark of the "Independent." The police too and the spies began to get troublesome, and by-and-by they got the better of the clubs altogether – the game was played out. It was in 1861 that the "Scotch Grey" was broken up. The year after that I commenced to keep some creature comforts for thirsty souls in my own dwelling-house in Saltmarket, and did so up till Whitsunday last year, as is well known to hundreds of respectable gentlemen, members of the police force, and others. To these persons I appeal if it is not the case that when in business on my own hook I kept a good article; although when working for others I have had to make a drop of brandy or a drop of gin on occasion. For the first of these I have taken a bottle of genuine Cognac, under proof, two bottles of raw grain whisky, 11 o.p., one bottle of Loch Katrine water, and poured them together through a funnel into a stone jar, and adding a gill of sherry to give it a better smell. In this way you can have four bottles brandy at a moderate cost – and quite good enough for lots of customers, too. Gin is not much asked for by Scotchmen, but in the clubs we had always to keep it for the English thieves. The best way to make gin is this: – Get 6d worth of juniper berries at the Apothecary Hall, and steep them for a week in water. Then put them into your jar and pour a gallon of raw grain 11 o.p. on top of them. In a day or two it will be as good gin as you require, and as you charge 6d a glass for it – at least we used to do – it pays. There is another little article we could never get on without, that it "rum colouring." There are some whiskies that if you reduce them too freely show a blue "scad," as we call it. Two or three drops of Jack-the-doctor will make them all right again. It is also very useful for imitating brandies and sherries.

I shall bring these remarks to a conclusion with a little story, and a true one. In 1867 a publican in the Wynd, who was a tin-smith to trade, came to me one Saturday and asked if I required any whisky. I said yes, if it was good enough and cheap enough. He pulled out of his pocket a small bottle, which I tasted, and said I would take either 5 or 10 gallons, but would like to know the price. He said it would be 5s less than I was paying for it. I said very well, send me either 5 or 10. That night, just after it got dark, a man knocked at our door and asked if Mr O'Neil was in. I told him I was the man, when he said that Mr So-and-so had sent him with what I ordered. I did not see any jar on his back, so I said "Where is it?" Says he, "I'll show you." I locked the door and brought him into the kitchen, where was none but our two selves. He then unbuttoned his monkey jacket, and to my surprise, I saw a tin pair of stays upon him – at least it was liker that than anything else. It was a vessel of tin-plate made to go round his body, for all the world the same as a pair of corsets, and fastened behind at two places. When he came into the kitchen he looked like a man of 16 or 17 stone, but when he had taken his stays off, I would say he was barely 10. I said "Where is the stuff?" He replied "It is here – bring a jar." I brought a 5-gallon jar, when he unscrewed a little cap from the top of a pipe at one corner of the stays, and poured out their contents into the jar. There was a little over the fill of the jar, which he and I discussed, and then he went away. After he was gone, I proceeded to reduce the stuff with two gallons of water. Next morning when I went to draw some of it, to my surprise, it looked the same as butter-milk and water mixed. Here was a go. There was nothing for it but to apply Jack-the-doctor, which I did freely, and sold

the blessed mixture as the best Irish whisky. The following week the man came back – without the stays this time – and asked if I wanted any more. I said to him "In the name of thunder, what stuff was yon you gave me?" "It was some of my own making," he replied, "didn't you know that I made it." "Indeed I did not." "Well then come over with me to Rose Street and I'll let you see." I went over the water with him to Rose Street, and into a house up two stairs. I saw nothing on entering that would give you an idea that such things were made there, but presently he pulled up two of the boards in the floor and showed me a portion of the worm of his still and of a pipe which conveyed the smoke from his fire up the chimney a short way. I asked him what he would do in the event of the authorities coming to the door and demanding admittance. "I'll show you" he says, and opens the window. Just outside the window I saw a rope hanging down from above, which rope he caught hold of, and jumping out swung himself over into another close, for all the world just like Myles-na-Coppaleen in the "Colleen Bawn." After he came back, I spoke again about his whisky turning white, when he told me that he had forgotten to tell me that I should reduce it with *hot* water; it was the cold water that had played the mischief with it. This I found afterwards to be correct. He also confessed to me that the chief ingredients he distilled were molasses and sour beer; still the price suited, and I gave him another order. There is another very good and cheap receipt for whisky, and if you would like to try it here are the proportions on a small scale. Two gills of the best whisky, 22 over proof, one gill of methylated spirits, 5 gills of water, and 2 drachms of sulphuric ether. This will give you eight gills in all, and not cost more than 1s 6d, and if you put a little rum colouring to it you can sell it as the best Irish at 4d a glass – and that pays. In some of the lower kick style of drums that I have known in my time, they added to the above a small portion of the stuff mentioned in the *Mail* by the name of fousel oil. I never interfered with it myself, but I know that it was put in to grip the mouth of the course Christians, and was strong enough to kill a priest.
– I am, etc.,
TOM O'NEIL,
Late Midnight Publican, of 18 Saltmarket.

So, there you have it; straight from the horse's mouth – methylated spirits, sulphuric ether, and added fusel-oil in shebeen whisky.

But what about public houses? Mr Smyth, Secretary of the Glasgow Wine, Spirit, and Beer Trade Association, would have been little bothered by such an honest revelation. It was *licensed* liquor-shops that came under his organisation's umbrella, and no publican had ever come forward to reveal his wrongful spirituous doings. As far as he was concerned, all his brethren were angels who could not possibly stoop so low as to tamper with whisky. Mr Smyth, like Professor Anderson, was living in cloud-cuckoo-land.

Most of the *'Mail's* articles and letters relating to the whisky disclosure were cut out of each day's newspaper back in 1872 and affixed to a scrap-book. This book of cuttings was gifted to the Mitchell Library twenty-five years later, in 1897. The donor is unknown. Whoever it was sensed the importance of the whole affair and wished to retain the gathered information for the benefit and interest of future generations.

However, there are some letters which are clearly part of the story but were somehow omitted from this scrap-book, and two of these are of some consequence. Something very peculiar was going on with Glasgow's public house whisky.

Sir, – It has been pretty clearly made out that we have been supplied with nothing but perfectly pure whisky, and so your analysis of Glasgow whisky falls to the ground as a tissue of falsehood from beginning to end. This is so far satisfactory, but it is merely the case as stated on behalf of the Wine, Beer, and Spirit Merchants' Association. Permit me to say, however, that there has been a great deal too much of mere assertion, and what is wanted now is evidence. I can supply two items, and I have no doubt that you will get scores more in a very short time. Two men, who had been working late on a Saturday night, went into a place which was literally crowded, to have a "taste" before going home. As it was near eleven o'clock, they drank their whisky at the counter and separated. One of them had scarcely reached home when he became sick, and remained so all night, all next day, and part of the succeeding night. He managed to his work, however, on Monday morning, and his first care when arriving there was to search for his companion of the preceding Saturday night. He was absent, nor did he manage to his work till after breakfast on Wednesday, when he appeared in a very emaciated condition, and declared that he had been sick, and had been purging a great deal from the time that he drank the whisky on Saturday night. The other item of evidence has scarcely the same physiological effects, but shows the nature of the liquid sometimes sold as whisky. I suppose you are aware that men occasionally get into such a condition that their hand becomes unsteady. Whether you are aware of that or not, such, however, is the case. Well, one whose hand had arrived at this unsteady point while bringing another glass to his mouth spilled some of the whisky on his linen. Wherever the liquid fell the linen was burned as if with vitriol. What have the wine and spirit trade advocates to say to these facts? Are they prepared to assert that whisky such as that analysed by Dr Gray is not sold in Glasgow? If not – and I believe they dare not say so – what is the reason for all the abuse they have been showering upon Dr Gray?

I am, etc.,

SPECTATOR[1]

The second, less dramatic, letter was published two days later.

Sir, – I rejoice that you took up the question of whisky adulteration in Glasgow. "Question," I say intentionally, for there has been a weak attempt to upset the conclusion stated in the *Mail's* analytical reports. However, no amount of virtuous indignation on the part of interested publicans, or of resolutions and counter analyses issuing from an association which cannot afford to be disinterested in this matter, will alter the general impression in the public mind regarding the badness of the whisky commonly sold. I once drank half a glass of whisky in a small publican's establishment in Glasgow. That was exactly five years ago. This small quantity of spirits went to my brain rapidly, and I felt stupid and irritable for twelve hours afterwards. Half a glass of good whisky would not have had the same bad effect. The accident served me as a "caution" ever since, and my reading has confirmed me in being cautious. ... [2]

It is difficult to understand how, or indeed why, such an obviously essential element of the whisky story could have been left out of the previously-mentioned scrap-book. Both letters were printed on the same day as others that *were* included, so they could not simply have been overlooked. Whoever compiled the book of cuttings deliberately excluded them, and in doing so retained what is in effect a biased record. One or two other less-notable letters were also excluded, several detailing the circumstances surrounding Tatlock's alleged – but then strongly repudiated – involvement in the detection of methyl alcohol in other whisky samples. It is therefore tempting to muse that the scrap-book was made up by someone siding with the publicans' camp, who wished to ignore any references to the poor quality whisky sold in some public houses, and who refused to accept the facts. We will never know who that person was.

The Why and Wherefore

Glasgow's mid-Victorian whisky problem was essentially one of adulteration, although other factors were also involved. The blending of whisky on a fairly large and organised scale was first carried out in the 1850s, and by 1872 the resulting tipple had grown considerably in popularity. Publicans were no doubt keen to cash-in on this new drinking trend and probably paid a bit more attention to their own 'House Special', at least in what it contained.

Unfortunately many lacked the necessary skills and, if not supplied by a wholesale merchant or distiller, the blend was made on the premises in a rather haphazard fashion with whiskies of varying age and quality being thrown together to form a unique mixture. If the resulting metamorphosis tasted more rough than ready, a huge range of substances could be added to smooth over any harshness. Prune wine, for example, was widely used for mellowing spirits and was possibly employed with some so-called 'blends'. We have already seen in Chapter Two that sherry wine, tartaric and acetic acids, sugar, pineapple and other fruit essences, tincture of prunes, acetic ether, oil of wine, spirit of nitrous ether, glycerine, and green tea were used to disguise the noxious flavour of new whisky, and you can be sure that many were also used in blends.

While prune wine and one or two other substances may have been regarded as acceptable by some members of the spirit trade, there was a real problem in knowing where the dividing-line between additives and adulterants lay, especially for the publican who merely dabbled. No rules existed to say what was permissable and what wasn't. The definition of whisky itself was somewhat ill-defined and it wasn't until 1908 that the question 'What is Whisky?' was officially addressed by the Government. However, although there may have been some confusion over what whisky was allowed to contain, it must again be stressed that adulteration was the main cause of the crisis and the word 'blend' was used in a cavalier manner to cover a multitude of sins. There was seldom any innocent experimenting involved in the practices executed by devious individuals.

Why, therefore, shouldn't an enterprising publican of low morals turn to methylated spirits or indeed any of the adulterants mentioned in the 'Mail's report? Well, one good reason is that it was illegal to use the former in any kind of beverage, although this wouldn't have been a barrier to some. Publicans were not just as virtuous as Mr Smyth would have us believe. Newspapers of the period carry numerous accounts of them being charged for selling alcohol on Sundays when they should have been closed, so if they were so inclined to break the law on this issue then it was no great step for them to further offend in the area of illicit drink. In addition, such was the profit-margin on beer that few publicans could hope to survive without adulterating, and skills learned in one medium were easily adapted to another. The adulteration of gin, brandy, and other spirituous liquors was well-documented, but it wasn't until the 'Mail grabbed the bull by the horns in 1872 that whisky was thrust into the limelight in Scotland.

As far back as 1855 when Professors Graham, Hofmann and Redwood submitted their report to the Inland Revenue on the viability of methylated spirits, it was stated that its addition to whisky would have to be guarded against – problems were foreseen even at this early stage. 'Methylated Whiskey' was beginning to surface in Ireland in early 1872, and reports were published in various periodicals detailing the gross adulteration in public houses in Belfast. There were many similarities between the great industrial cities of Belfast and Glasgow, and to imagine that the former was alone in encountering such malpractises would be folly.

With most of whisky's adulterants their use was necessary to add a false strength, taste and colour to a spirit greatly diluted with water. It was no different to other forms of adulteration involving food and drink in that means had to be found to restore the original properties of a product that had been expanded with a cheaper material. After the addition of water, methylated spirits or 'finish' would have been added to boost the reduced alcoholic strength. The finding of turpentine was something of a surprise as its function is not too obvious. However, John Mitchell's *Treatise on the Falsifications of Food*, dating to 1848, informs us that oil of turpentine was used, along with other items, in gin to disguise dilution by adding a pungency which detracted from the watery taste. Colouring agents might have been added, although not always – a number of the 'Mail's samples were colourless – along with chemicals to keep the spirit clear and to maintain the property of 'beading' – where the spirit hangs 'in pearly drops or beads on the side of the glass containing it.' The final mixture would be a chemical cocktail that was a whisky blend in name alone.

Is it Safe?

The Inland Revenue were understandably quite concerned when Glasgow erupted in an explosion of adulterated whisky. Behind the scenes, and with little fuss, on the 15th October 1872, they collected samples from public houses in the city and had six of them analysed in their own laboratory. They could detect nothing out of the ordinary. Their results were not made public at that time.

On the 14th November the publican's champion William Smyth wrote to the Inland Revenue to ask for a copy of their findings. On the 6th December Smyth's letter and the Inland Revenue's reply were published in the *Glasgow Herald* and then again in a handbill which was circulated among the publicans of Glasgow. The leaflet started thus ...

> To Members of the Association of Wine and Spirit Merchants in Glasgow, and the Public generally.
> The directors consider it expedient that the utmost publicity should be given to the following correspondence, which clearly and indisputably proves to be groundless the accusations of adulteration of whisky so prominently published in the columns of the *North British Daily Mail* of 25th and 30th September last, and which provoked much sensational comment, universally prejudicial to respectable retailers and dealers in spirits. The critical exposition of Mr R. R. Tatlock, F.R.S.E., F.C.S., analytical chemist, Glasgow, on the instructions of the association, of the fallacies contained in the *Mail's* report and analyses, satisfied every interested newspaper reader of the absurdity of the whole statements; ...

Quite clearly Mr Smyth was having a field day, rubbing salt into wounds and defending his own interests – if adulteration was proved, it would reflect badly on his organisation's ability to keep their members under control.

None of this escaped the notice of Doctor Cameron, the 'Mail's editor, who promptly wrote to the Inland Revenue to find out when exactly they had taken their samples. It was as he had expected; the 15th October was practically three weeks after the 'Mail's initial report.

On the 23rd December, Cameron's final words on the subject were published. He made the point that in that intervening three week period Glasgow's publicans cleaned up their act. They might adulterate, but they were not daft. With all the hullabaloo that followed the first and second reports, and the public outcry that developed and gathered momentum, any publican guilty of such malpractices must have anticipated a visit from someone in authority and would immediately have got rid of any tampered goods and reverted to the upright worker of Mr. Smyth's dreams. Consequently, when the Inland Revenue *did* take samples, no adulteration was found, and it's hardly surprising.

Much has been said by critics of the *'Mail's* report on the apparent inconsistencies and inaccuracies in Doctor Gray's analyses. Some of these criticisms are possibly true, but then attention to detail seems to be something that frequently fell by the wayside with chemists of the period. In previous chapters we have witnessed time and time again the total disagreements that followed the analytical strivings of eminent scientists, not to mention the nonsense that spouted from the pen of one university professor. Doctor Gray was not alone in making an occasional and minor blunder.

Did he detect methyl alcohol by chemical means? I firmly believe that he did, although today's chemists would dispute this. There were a number of methods available in the 1860s and early 1870s, but all were unreliable, and it wasn't until around 1875 that it could be properly detected in an ethylic mixture. Nevertheless, although the method used by Gray may be said to be unworkable by today's standards, his familiarity with techniques used to detect miniscule quantities of other substances leads me to suspect that he may well have successfully applied the test, paying attention to every detail so as to wring the method of its total worth. Even if Tatlock was correct in his opinion that methylic spirit could not be thus detected, it is certainly not a reflection on Gray's ability as a chemist, but more on the state of analytical science that then existed.

He did *not* fashion a set of results from out of the top of his 'over-imaginative' head, as suggested by one sceptic, and did in fact do his damnedest to carry out a thorough scientific investigation into the samples he was given. He made use of recognised techniques as described by established and renowned chemists, and even after countless rounds of dissension with Tatlock was still able to defend his results convincingly. No man could have done more.

Gray was a young man. He may have overlooked one or two details in his haste to submit his results, but you can be assured that on the whole he confronted the challenge with the same degree of thought and precision to which he was accustomed when working with Professor Rainy on matters of a forensic nature.

In 1874, one-hundred-and-thirty-six people died of diphtheria in Glasgow. Doctor James St. Clair Gray was one of them. It was a short four-day illness, Gray spending his last few days at the family home at 15 Newton Terrace where his father did what little he could to treat his eldest son. He died on 11th December, at the age of twenty-seven, around two years after Glasgow's great whisky debate ended.

With both Tatlock – who was indeed a most respected analyst – and the Excise failing to detect any serious adulteration shortly after the 'Mail's report in 1872, the authorities simply refused to believe that Glasgow had such a serious drink problem; as far as they were concerned, the mystery had never existed. Of course there would have been a few who knew exactly what the true state of affairs was, but they had conducted their tests and nothing further could be done. Tatlock enforced the former view rather cruelly in 1898 when, as one of the city's public analysts, he gave his thoughts on the general state of Scottish whisky. In a letter which was published in Glasgow's *Sanitary Department Report*, he described his own experiences in whisky sampling and analysis and stated that 'of all the hundreds of thousands of samples of whisky which have been purchased under every variety of circumstance during the last quarter of a century, and submitted to the Public Analysts for analysis, I am not aware of one instance in which it has been alleged that the spirit was of a noxious character ...'[3] It is hard to know what Tatlock is saying here. He may be giving Doctor Gray the benefit of the doubt – when the 1872 tests were done, Glasgow did not then have a Public Analyst – his 'quarter of a century' date range falling just short, perhaps conveniently, of the 1872 events. Or he may be further debasing Gray's good name by refusing to even acknowledge that the mystery had ever occurred. In another sentence which can be taken a number of ways and which I feel certain is a direct reference to his battle with Doctor Gray, he says: 'anything that

In the late nineteenth century Glasgow's spirit merchants did their damnedest to dispel any remaining notion that the city's whisky was still on the rough side. This blend used the fountain which commemorates the completion of Glasgow's first public water-supply as a symbol of purity. (*Mitchell Library*).

savours of mystery dies hard.' Considering Gray's ultimate fate, I find this comment most distasteful.

In the Victorian decades that followed the 1872 controversy, the whisky industry gradually introduced various measures to help quell public fears. Promotional material featured testimonies from eminent chemists who proclaimed that the spirit was good and wholesome and free from fusel-oil and other noxious ingredients. Emphasis was placed on the age of the whisky and the resulting lack of those substances that gave newly-distilled spirit its harshness. Some, like the 'Cantire Blend', played on the toxic aspect by stating that they were 'thoroughly safe', as did the 'Kelvingrove Whisky' which was advertised as 'pure'. There was even one blend named 'The Safety Old Highland Whisky'. A lot of this was aimed at putting their customers' minds at rest in relation

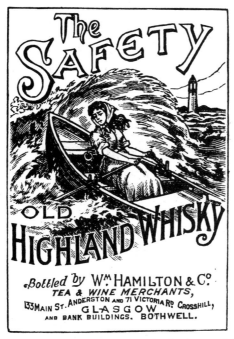

This whisky was presumably quite safe to drink! (*Mitchell Library*).

to the continuing debate over fusel-oil and its toxicity (a debate that eventually led to the legal requirement that all whisky *had* to be matured for at least three years before being put on the market), but the issue of adulteration was obviously lying just under the surface.

Metallic capsules were fitted on bottles so as to prevent tampering, and much thought was put into bottle-label design so that the product of a particular distiller or merchant could be easily identified. In this way the man in the street could be assured of the quality and authenticity of his favourite tipple. Nevertheless, some public house whisky remained open to the devious tinkerings of anyone who cared to defraud the unsuspecting drinker, a fact that is amply proved by the Leith methylated spirits cases that were briefly reported in *The Northern Provision Trade Journal* in September 1885. As this fine periodical said – a flood of light was being shed on the secrets of the Scottish whisky trade …

It would seem that the practice of mixing the vile wood-spirit with ordinary coarse strong Scottish whisky is of wider range than the

161

authorities at first imagined. The flavour which some of the coarse Scottish whiskies possess help to disguise the unpalatable taste of the methylitic spirit, and thus assists unscrupulous persons.

Doctor Tatlock no doubt knew nothing of this when he made his sweeping and insensitive statement in 1898.

The Essential Press

In the mid-Victorian period the Government was really *trying* to come to grips with a multitude of social problems. Unfortunately statutes took quite some time to filter through the parliamentary system, and even once passed they often needed alteration so as to have the desired effect. In addition, blinkered foresight inevitably led to unanticipated backlashes as witnessed in the shebeen increase following the 1853 Public House Act. In some ways the Government was to blame for the widespread adulteration of food and drink. They did little to protect the poorer classes, and when forced into action the result was often ineffectual. As far as spirits are concerned, the continuing duty increase – and especially that which took place in the years immediately following the same 1853 Act – gave the publican (who was already struggling to survive) an added incentive to dilute and adulterate.

Newspapers played a vital role, as they still do today, in examining areas of social neglect in which the Government refused to peer. The *North British Daily Mail* carried out many investigations for the good of the people, often exposing hitherto unknown or little talked-about practices that circulated in the working man's world. Some of their major exposés played a key role in bringing such matters to the attention of the Government, and it was high profile news coverage of this nature that at times led to bills being read in Parliament. Their Baby-Farming and Truck System probes come into this category.

The 'Mail's public-spirited reports did not stop with *The Mysteries of Glasgow Whisky*, and they went on to look at the adulteration of tea in Glasgow. As was typical for the period, most of the analysed samples were laced with all manner of substances that definitely weren't tea. Adulteration was rife, in *everything*. The 'Mail most certainly was not in the business of sensationalism.

Little did Doctor Gray realise when first agreeing to assist Doctor

Cameron that he would become involved in something which, in my view, should be a well-recorded part of Scottish history. The story of whisky does not start in the countryside with peat, crystal clear water and fields of golden barley, and end at the distillery. It encompasses the whole sequence of events leading up to and including the moment when a glass is raised to lips and the contents savoured. The sale of whisky in public houses is therefore very much a part of this story, and in 1872 that sold in Glasgow was found to be of such poor quality that the good name of Scotland's national drink took a severe knock.

Sadly, but perhaps understandably, the whisky industry takes no pleasure in recalling such episodes from its past, and little will be found on the subject of adulteration within the plethora of books that lie on library and bookshop shelves. As far as the industry and those in authority are concerned, Glasgow's mystery did not take place. I can assure you it did.

Today's whisky industry has no record of the events of 1872. In hiding behind the ghosts of Tatlock, Anderson, and the like, they are disowning an important part of their heritage, and one which deserves its proper place in the annals of time.

I take great pleasure in putting the whole story where it rightly belongs.

Reference Sources

Chapter 2

1 *The Food Journal*, 1 August 1871, p 311.

2 *ibid*, 1 June 1872, p 163.

3 *The Lancet*, 23 August 1856, p 229.

4 *ibid*, 13 November 1858, p 504.

5 Arthur Hill Hassall, *Food and its Adulterations* (1855) p 460.

6 Arthur Hill Hassall, *Food: Its Adulterations, and the Methods for Their Detection* (1876) p 837.

7 *The Food Journal*, 1 August 1871, p 312.

8 *The Analyst*, 1877, p 56.

9 *The Tricks of the Trade* (1856) p 53. Located in Glasgow University Library's Special Collections section, No. BG 59-n.13.

10 *The Analyst*, 1883, p 260.

11 *The Tricks of the Trade* (1856) p 59.

12 *The Analyst*, 1878, p 149.

13 *ibid*, 1877, p 117.

14 *ibid*, 1878, p 353.

15 *ibid*, 1879, p 36.

16 *The Food Journal*, 1 December 1870, p 586.

17 *The Analyst*, 1877, p 117. The Inland Revenue had a laboratory at Somerset House.

18 Hassall (1876) *op. cit.*, pp 841-848.

19 Chemist's recipe book (1870s). Located in Glasgow University Business Archives, No. UGD/209/1.

20 *The Analyst*, 1877, p117.

21 *The Food Journal*, 1 April 1870, p 168.

22 *The Lancet*, 8 November 1856, p 518.

23 *The Food Journal*, 1 August 1871, p 313.

24 A. Normandy, *The Commercial Hand-book of Chemical Analysis* (1875) p 84.

25 *The Food Journal*, 1 July 1870, pp 295-299.

26 *ibid*, 1 August 1870, pp 364-366.

27 *ibid*, 1 October 1872, p 331.

28 *Tobacco Talk and Smokers' Gossip* (1886) p 53.

29 Arthur Hill Hassall, *Adulterations Detected or Plain Instructions for the Discovery of Frauds in Food and Medicine* (1861) pp 14-16.

30 *The Chemist & Druggist*, 15 June 1876, p 225.

31 Normandy, *op. cit.*, p54.

32 A *Practical Treatise on Brewing* (1806) p 8. Located in Glasgow University Library, No. Y7-a.7.

33 *The Tricks of the Trade* (1856) p 100.

34 Hassall (1876) *op. cit.*, p 696.

35 56 Geo III c 58. 'An Act to repeal an Act made in the Fifty first Year of His Present Majesty, for allowing the Manufacture and Use of a Liquor prepared from Sugar for colouring Porter.' (1816)

36 Hassall (1855) *op. cit.*, p 628.

37 Robert Hunt, *Ure's Dictionary of Arts, Manufactures, and Mines* (1878) p 875.

38 Hassall (1876) *op. cit.*, p 695.

39 *ibid*. p 694.

40 Hassall (1855) *op. cit.*, p 633.

41 *The Tricks of the Trade* (1856) p 102.

42 *The Lancet*, 12 September 1857, p 283.

43 Hassall (1876) *op. cit.*, p 696.

44 *The Tricks of the Trade* (1856) p 99.

45 *ibid*, p 119.

46 Normandy, *op. cit.*, p 82.

47 *The Analyst*, 1878, p 149.

48 Hassall (1876) *op. cit.*, p 810.

49 *ibid*, p 813.

50 *ibid*, p 818.

51 *ibid*, p 805.

52 Normandy, *op. cit.*, p 84.

53 *The Food Journal*, 1 August 1873, p 279.

54 *The Victualling Trades' Review*, March 1891.

55 Normandy, *op. cit.*, p 83.

56 *The Scottish Wine, Spirit and Beer Trades' Review*, 31 May 1887.

57 Hunt, *op. cit.*, p 948.

58 *The Tricks of the Trade*, pp 123-124.

59 William Logan, *The Moral Statistics of Glasgow* (1849) p 36.

60 *Report of the Commissioners of Her Majesty's Inland Revenue on the Inland Revenue;* year ending 31 March 1872.

61 *The Food Journal*, 1 December 1870, p 561.

Chapter 3

1 *Glasgow Herald*, 23 February 1872.

2 *The Food Journal*, 1 October 1873, p 359.

3 *The Pharmaceutical Journal*, 20 April 1872, p 851.

4 *Glasgow Herald*, 24 April 1872.

5 *The Pharmaceutical Journal*, April 1870, pp 648-649.

6 *Glasgow Medical Journal*, February 1871.

7 *Glasgow Herald*, 31 October 1872.

8 *North British Daily Mail*, 28 September 1872.

9 *ibid*, 1 October 1872.

10 *ibid*, 1 October 1872.

11 *ibid*, 2 October 1872.

Chapter 4

1 John A. Monick, *Alcohols – Their Chemistry, Properties and Manufacture* (1968) p 89.

2 Daniel McCallum, *Edifying Information Concerning the Working Classes in Glasgow* (1889) p. 14.

3 Charles Simmonds, *Alcohol – Its Properties, Chemistry, and Industrial Applications* (1919) p 290.

4 *Report on the Supply of Spirit of Wine, Free from Duty, for Use in the Arts and Manufactures, addressed to the Chairman of Inland Revenue, by Professors Graham, Hofmann and Redwood*, 27 April 1855, p 1.

5 *A Return of Licenses Granted for the Making of Methylated Spirits Under the Act 18 & 19 Vict. c38.* (1856(326)LV. 575).

6 James Stirling, *Failure of the Forbes Mackenzie Act* (1859) p 31.

7 *Report on the Supply of Spirit of Wine, op. cit.*, p 12.

8 *The Pharmaceutical Journal*, July 1866, p 3.

9 *ibid*, July 1866, p 41.

10 *ibid*, August 1866, p 91.

11 *ibid*, August 1866, p 90.

12 *ibid*, August 1866, p 89.

13 *ibid*, April 1867, p 565.

14 *ibid*, October 1866, p 213.

15 *29 & 30 Vict. c64.* 'An Act to Amend the Laws Relating to the Inland Revenue.' (1866) Clause 9.

16 *The Pharmaceutical Journal*, October 1866, p 256.

17 *ibid*, June 1870, p 749.

18 *ibid*, June 1870, p 750.

Chapter 5

1 *The Pharmaceutical Journal*, February 1870, p 495.

2 Chemist's recipe book (1870s). Located in Glasgow University Business Archives, No. UGD/209/1.

3 *The Mercantile World*, 1 March 1879, p 74.

4 Stirling, *op. cit.*, pp 16-17.

5 *The Pharmaceutical Journal*, April 1870, p 631.

6 *ibid*, October 1866, p 262.

7 *The Scottish Wine, Spirit and Beer Trades' Review*, 24 May 1887.

8 *The Pharmaceutical Journal*, February 1867, p 485.

9 *ibid*, 20 April 1872, pp 851-852.

10 *The Chemist & Druggist*, 15 November 1879, p 491.

11 *The Food Journal*, 1 June 1872, p 193.

12 *ibid*, 1 November 1872, p 397.

13 *The Pharmaceutical Journal*, April 1870, p 649.

14 *North British Daily Mail*, 8 January 1867. (The Finish Trade.)

15 *The Scottish Wine, Spirit and Beer Trades' Review*, 20 September 1887 p 260.

16 *Dumfries & Galloway Standard & Advertiser*, 22 February 1888. (Letters to the Editor.)

17 *North British Daily Mail*, 15 October 1872.

Chapter 6

1 M. Anne Crowther and Brenda White, *On Soul and Conscience – the Medical Expert and Crime* (1988) p 20.

2 *North British Daily Mail*, 17 October 1872.

3 *ibid*, 25 October 1872.

4 *The Bailie*, No. 1352, 14 September 1898.

5 *North British Daily Mail*, 1 October 1872, p 4, col 4.

6 *The Bailie*, 30 October 1872.

7 *ibid*, 6 November 1872.

Chapter 7

1 J. Smith, *The Grievances of the Working Classes; and the Pauperism and Crime of Glasgow* (1846) p 20

2 ibid, *p. 21.*

3 'Shadow', *op. cit.*, p 98.

4 *ibid*, p. 145.

5 Smith, *op. cit.*, p 27.

6 William Logan, *The Moral Statistics of Glasgow* (1849) p 62.

7 *ibid*, p 11.

8 James Stirling, *Failure of the Forbes Mackenzie Act* (1859) p 9.

9 *ibid*, p 11.

10 *Public Houses' Act Conference. Testimonies and Statistics* (1855) p84. Located in Glasgow University Library, No. Y10-m.3.

11 Stirling, *op. cit.*, pp 27-28.

12 City of Glasgow Police; *Criminal Returns.*

13 Daniel McCallum, *Edifying Information Concerning the Working Classes in Glasgow* (1889) p 14.

14 Stirling, *op. cit.*, pp 14-15.

15 City of Glasgow Police; *Criminal Returns.*

16 *North British Daily Mail*, 19 June 1871.

17 *The Victualling Trades' Review*, 1 June 1893, p 138.

18 *ibid*, 15 March 1894, pp 114-115.

19 *ibid*, 1 June 1893, p 138.

20 *North British Daily Mail*, 22 July 1869, p 4.

21 *ibid*, 29 July 1869, p 5.

22 *ibid*.

23 *ibid*.

Chapter 8

1 *North British Daily Mail*, 29 October 1872.

2 *ibid*, 31 October 1872.

3 *Glasgow Sanitary Department Report*, year ending 31 December 1897, pp 17-21.

Bibliography

Location reference numbers have been included for only a few of those listed below; most of the material will be available at any one of the main public or university reference libraries in either Glasgow or Edinburgh.

BOOKS, PAMPHLETS, REPORTS AND RETURNS

Accum, F., A Treatise on Adulterations of Food and Culinary Poisons (1820). Glasgow University Library Special Collections No. Ar-c. 7, 29.

Anon, A Practical Treatise on Brewing (1806). Glasgow University Library No. Y7-a.7.

Anon, The Tricks of the Trade in the Adulterations of Food and Physic (1856). Glasgow University Library Special Collections No. BG 59-n.13.

Anon, Doings of a Notorious Glasgow Shebeener. (Known to be written by Tom O'Neil and first published, in reduced form, in 1872.)

British Pharmacopoeia (1864).

Crowther, M. A. and White, B., On Soul and Conscience – the Medical Expert and Crime (1988).

City of Glasgow Police – Criminal Returns (1857-1878).

City of Glasgow Sanitary Department – Instructions (1870).

City of Glasgow Sanitary Department – Report (1870-1897).

Gray, James St. Clair, An Analysis of 143 Cases of Poisoning with Strychnia (1871).

Gray, James St. Clair, Strychnia (1872).

Gunn, Neil M., Whisky and Scotland (1935).

Hassall, Arthur Hill, Food and its Adulterations (1855).

Hassall, Arthur Hill, Adulterations Detected or Plain Instructions for the Discovery of Frauds in Food and Medicine (1861). Glasgow University Library Special Collections No. BG 59-L6.

Hassall, Arthur Hill, Food, its Adulterations, and the Methods for Their Detection (1876).

Hunt, Robert, *Ure's Dictionary of Arts, Manufactures, and Mines* (1878).

Logan, William, *The Moral Statistics of Glasgow* (1849).

McCallum, Daniel, *Edifying Information Concerning the Working Classes in Glasgow* (1889).

Macleod, Kenneth M., *The City Sanitary Organisation: Its Aids and Obstacles* (1872).

Mitchell, John, *Treatise on the Falsifications of Food* (1848).

Monick, John A., *Alcohols, their Chemistry, Properties and Manufacture* (1968).

Normandy, A., *The Commercial Hand-book of Chemical Analysis* (1875).

Paton, Jeffrey, *Additives, Adulterants and Contaminants in Beer* (1989).

Post Office Directories for the City of Glasgow.

Public-Houses' Act Conference. Testimonies and Statistics (1855). Glasgow University Library No. Y10-m.3.

Report on the Supply of Spirit of Wine, free from Duty, for Use in the Arts and Manufactures – addressed to the Chairman of Inland Revenue, by Professors Graham, Hofmann and Redwood (1855).

Report of the Commissioners of Her Majesty's Inland Revenue on the Inland Revenue (1872 and 1878).

Report from the Select Committee on British and Foreign Spirits (1890).

Final Report of the Royal Commission on Whiskey and other Potable Spirits (1909).

A Return of Licenses Granted for the Making of Methylated Spirits under the Act 18 & 19 Vict.c.38 (1856 and 1857).

Saintsbury, George, *Notes on a Cellar-Book* (1920).

'Shadow', *Midnight Scenes and Social Photographs* (1858).

Sillet, S. W., *Illicit Scotch* (1965).

Simmonds, Charles, *Alcohol, its Production, Properties, Chemistry, and Industrial Applications* (1919).

Smart, James, *Report on the Working of the Public House Acts in the City of Glasgow for 1856* (1857).

Smith, J., *The Grievances of the Working Classes; and the Pauperism and Crime of Glasgow* (1846).

Stirling, James, *Failure of the Forbes Mackenzie Act* (1859).

Stockton, John, *Victorian Bottles* (1981).

Strang, John, *Glasgow and its Clubs* (1857).

Ure, Andrew, *The Revenue in Jeopardy from Spurious Chemistry Demonstrated in Researches upon Wood-Spirit and Vinous-Spirit* (1843).

NEWSPAPERS AND PERIODICALS

The Analyst (1877-1883).

The Bailie (1872-1906).

The British Medical Journal (1872).

The Chemist & Druggist (1876-1879).

Dublin Journal of Medical Science (1872-1875).

Dumfries & Galloway Standard & Advertiser (1888).

The Food Journal (1870-1874).

Glasgow Herald (1858 and 1872).

Glasgow Medical Journal (1870-1874).

The Lancet (1855-1860).

The Mercantile World (1879).

North British Daily Mail (1869-1872).

The Pharmaceutical Journal (1866-1872).

The Quarterly Review (1855).

The Scottish Wine, Spirit and Beer Trades' Review (1887).

Trade Marks Journal (1876-1976).

The Victualling Trades' Review (1893-1894).

Index